# FOLLOW YOUR CALLING

I'M LIVING
MY DREAM

A WORKBOOK FOR THOSE WHO REALLY WANT TO
IMPROVE THEIR LIFE

ALEXANDER TEETZ

# A RARE WARE LIFE MANAGEMENT BOOK

Published by RARE WARE Medienverlag (Publishers)

D-22335 Hamburg

www.rare-ware.info

First International Edition, Hamburg, Germany, 2013

*RARE WARE can bring authors to your live event.*
*For more information contact mail@rare-ware.info*

Cover Design and Layout: www.andreakelb.de

Translation: Sylvia Ondaza, TX, USA with Alexander Teetz, HH, Germany

Printing: www.lightningsource.com

ISBN 978-3-942791-06-9

I dedicate this book
especially to my loving wife Kim,
our son Jason, my parents and all others
who have supported me along my way.

# THE AUTHOR

Alexander Teetz (Sagittarius), born in 1959, is a coach, consultant, trainer and author. He is a regular lecturer at several institutions for the further education of adolescents and adults in the fields of communication, application training and personal development. He is married to choreographer Kim Moke and they reside in Hamburg, with their son Jason.

"life angel"® Alex. supports institutions and individuals ("unclear or unhappy") in occupational situations or in their private life to help them discover their individual qualities, needs and strengths in order to improve their self-assessment, their ability to communicate and to act responsibly. His ethical principle is based on the "categorical imperative" of the German philosopher, Immanuel Kant (1724 – 1804).

In 1995, after his apprenticeship as an international trader and several successful positions in the sales and management of various businesses, he founded, as part of his personal vocation, RARE WARE® Life Management. Here everything revolves around the human being, his society and the environment. As an author and motivational speaker, he defines himself as a promoter and catalyst who likes to inform in an entertaining manner, following the principle of "personal empowerment". Alex. wants to inspire people, to actively do the best for themselves to improve their individual as well as the common life-quality based on a platform of Love, Joy and Respect.

In 2012, together with an American and a Russian, he founded the charitable "life angel foundation", for the support of independent first class education, for talent without money. This concept promotes the collaboration of "Young" and "Old", including the possibility of living together in a spacious multi-generation "Spiritual Village".

# TABLE OF CONTENTS

# DEAR READERS

My former editor advised me it would be best to place this page behind the preface because the text is somewhat stilted and could confuse interested readers regarding the further contents. He is correct in his assumption but I can't help myself! So, don't let this confuse you. If necessary, simply skip over this page. Further on in the book it will be more down-to-earth. I developed the following information 1996 after investigating into Corporate Identity for use in a Hamburg publishing house in which I was sales and marketing manager. This proved to be too discerning for them. I was astonished and had sworn to myself to have this printed at the beginning of all my books. In addition to the persiflage of obligatory warnings on cigarette packaging I would like to see this statement on all video media:

Research on the brain has proven that "Knowledge and Education" are formed from referential information processing, that means through structuring of information and judgment development. Reading is a referential process. Frequent readers control a framework in their mind that enables referential information processing and therefore the inclination to emotional and intellectual capacities such as abstraction capacity, command of the language, imagination activity and creativity.

Due its importance in the development of structuring and abstraction capacity, reading is the basic cultural technique for competent utilization of all media. Reading is the basis for individual qualification. Language and literacy are necessary requirements for active participation in our life's modern, complex society. Empirical social research has proven that readers command an exceptional amount of personality strength and social competence. They are more confident in their judgment and have more perseverance in their actions than the non-reader. Encouraging people to read is in the interest of democratic thinking!

SURGEON GENERAL'S WARNING:

READING ENDANGERS THE PROCESS OF SENILITY
GIVING UP READING REDUCES THE RISK OF A
COMPLEX THINKING PROCESS

# PREFACE

Every person has his very own individual quality, his personal potential to sustainable happiness in life! It doesn't matter if you are "poor" or "rich", "smart" or "dumb"; everyone searches at one point for an occupation with meaning and purpose as an essential part of a happy and fulfilling life. This book is based on this knowledge! Unfortunately, only a few are successful in their search because many have already let themselves be confused and misled in their choice of occupation by rational and/or materialistic motives. They suppress their instincts, as well as skills and talents acquired at an early age. It is then easy to become engaged in a role behavior that is a far cry from their "calling" and a fulfilling life. The result creates unhappy people who make unfortunate decisions in their professional and private lives, for themselves and for others. This also influences the worldwide quality of life negatively!

One day I started thinking consciously about life in general, my life and the lives of almost everyone I knew or I had heard about somehow, somewhere and at sometime. I couldn't help it, I simply am interested in people. While I had had a relatively carefree childhood, I realized as I grew older how many serious problems mankind had overall and I just had to do something about it. I think it all started when I was sixteen in my Philosophy class whereby my interest was certainly piqued by my attractive, pleasant-smelling teacher. Moreover, I later had a very good German achievement course teacher who always understood how to sharpen our senses for all possible communicative and social aspects through varied literature.

At this time, I was also confronted for the first time with the „categorical imperative", which I meanwhile have integrated into my own life philosophy and on which all desired values and goals in this book are based on:

## "ACT ACCORDINGLY SO THAT THE MAXIM OF YOUR WILLINGNESS AT ANY TIME CAN BE REGARDED AT THE SAME TIME AS A PRINCIPLE OF UNIVERSAL LAW, WITHOUT CONTRADICTION."

Immanuel Kant, German Philosopher, 1724 – 1804

There are so many people on this earth, they surround us and are constantly increasing in numbers. Many people who like me, when really interested in a subject want to know something precisely and can only believe what they can comprehend logically in detail. I therefore began to search for insight and the more I sought, the more I found. The more I compared, the more parallels I was able to recognize. At the same time I assessed that all people are searching for a purpose and fulfillment in their life so they can gain a long-term satisfying feeling of self-esteem and use this as the groundwork to develop true joy of living. The desire for this becomes greater with the process of advanced self-awareness and increasing life experience. Often a certain traumatic event in life drives a person to find insight and fulfillment in life. Nevertheless, only a few people have the ability and strength to take the required action in this direction although the potential to do so definitely exists in everyone. Only a small percentage of people manage to create long-term good fortune and happiness in life. It is usually those who have gone their own way from the beginning, created their own goals, searching for solutions within themselves and those who concentrate on their own individual strengths and overall basic values. In addition, they also have the capacity of sober observance, and „Introspection" in connection with utmost (self) honesty, but also endurance, perseverance and above all, self-discipline. For most of us, this a difficult task, without impetus or support from outside. There's a reason for the old proverb „Self-insight is the first step to improvement"!

I had the good fortune to win this insight when I was almost 35 in a guided clearing process during the course of a public workshop that my younger sister had persuaded me to go to. It finally became clear to me what I needed to do with the qualities I had acquired in life in order to achieve long-term good fortune and meaning. As it was, all these ingredients were already "simmering" in me. They only had to be awakened and organized initially. Although I was at that time the managing director of a designer furniture company and led a comfortable life there was something missing in my life that I was not able to describe verbally. My occupation at that time simply did not offer me the opportunity to unfold my qualities and demands on my life fully.

From this key experience that weekend the concept of my current RARE WARE Life Management emerged. Suddenly one insight followed the other, like a flower that slowly blossoms and becomes more beautiful. "RARE WARE", which I created, was originally intended as a simple to understand international synonym and had been present in my head for several years as the symbol for the valuable and precious individual. The „Life management" pertains to the clever handling of our life – like a good manager helps its business to a long and successful life.

This is exactly my task! It had become clear to me: I want to contribute in improving the quality of life for all living things by taking a stand, revealing possibilities, setting examples and motivating people to believe in themselves and their own individual path based on their valid human values – to follow their calling. I know this is possible, because I am living this experience. I have learned my entire life to think positively and lovingly, for already as a child my dreams and fantasies were always supported and encouraged. I was loved by my parents and was allowed to learn: Whatever you can imagine, you can achieve. Everything is basically possible!

This book, developed from my personal life experience in search of my calling, involving contact with people of all age groups and based on my present work, is only a means of finding the way. It is addressed to everyone who wants to make more out of their life and their (our) world; those who still have dreams and are prepared to start with themselves as the basis for general improvement of quality of life on earth. The contents enable all age groups access to a more spiritual, therefore less materialistic attitude towards work, occupation and whatever accounts for personal success. In this manner, the related exercises form a universal basic scheme to finding personal development. They are especially effective for young, independent people before they enter the professional world and for all people who sense the desire and will to change their life, no matter what age. The timing will always be right!

# 01 | PEOPLE AND LABOR

Our profession, our work, our job – whatever we may call it – has a specific, increasing influence on our lives from a certain age onwards. How much it will affect us, depends mainly on us. Only we ourselves can considerably control what to make of our lives and how far we will allow others to have an impact on our life. Eventually we will determine what it is, whether we call it a profession, a hobby, sports, charity, the arts or just leisure. We are all looking for this one purpose in life. The purpose we want and are supposed to serve in terms of common welfare, so life will be worth living, individually and in general. The earlier we engage ourselves with this matter, the earlier we will find more fulfillment in life. Of course, there is more to living a satisfying life than having a satisfying occupation. But this profession, in whatever form, is a very important component of life and the more it becomes a vocational calling, the more intense we experience joy and passion in life.

The majority of us grow up as children in a more or less non-materialistic carefree environment and only consciously experience at a certain age that what they may have felt was sufficient is not really sufficient for the standards of others at all. We thus develop standards that we might never have required if we hadn't compared ourselves with others' standard to begin with. However, as soon as we do compare these, most people stop being satisfied and the obvious comparative values become the visible ones. It first begins in kindergarten, but at the latest becomes evident in school when for instance, the individual outfit is judged because society (regarded superficially) is simply inclined to being materialistic. If we are lucky, our parents will be able to keep up financing whatever is necessary, but if not we, and or our parents will experience frustration in this materialistic comparison.

At any rate, we have experienced the first categorization of life regarding material priorities, which usually increases the older we become. This can occur particularly at the ages between ten and fifty years, when we are increasingly judged by our environment, based on material values. For example, the value of the working force in some enterprises. If we are not inheritors of an enterprise fed with material abundance, who can mainly finance his identification process from a well filled bank account (often the most unsatisfying form, by the way), we are obliged to realize that if we want to live a certain lifestyle, we will sooner or later have to finance this identification process ourselves somehow. Either as an assistant to an entrepreneur on his way to personal fulfillment or, better, yet be your own entrepreneur or perhaps even a balanced mix of both. That's why our profession has such an important impact on our lives, because we often primarily try to finance our consumer-oriented bliss due to a lack of life experience and tend to look for happiness in the wrong places and/or try to create happiness using the wrong means.

However, this desperately sought-after bliss or happiness only develops if we do what we enjoy doing in the long run and what satisfies us within, far beyond material consumption and frustrating comparison. That is the point when material circumstances become secondary. Recognizing meaningful goals in life, the inner security of making the right decision and the conscious enjoyment of being on the right track are the exciting ingredients which add spice to our life and enable us to fully enjoy it. Over and over again, surveys have shown that only a third of all employees find joy in their occupation. Actually, many have turned away from their work inside because they find no enjoyment in their jobs and often just stay for financial reasons – to finance the leftover frazzle of their lives when they're not working.

Today, every fifth office clerk as well as every fourth worker retires early from (nomen est omen) their working life. Approximately ninety percent of these people retire due to occupational disability caused by illness. And more than thirty percent of those retire due to psychic (!) reasons. Only ten percent retire early from work due to disability caused by accidents. The rest, however, approximately a fifth of all employees (those are the people who work for others), become ill due to their job stress causing them to become incapable of carrying out their job or any other type of job. These are "broken" people. Is it perhaps possible that their jobs brought on their illnesses? Yes!

The sad news is that this is becoming more common because the world is becoming increasingly more materialistic. People often choose a job based on the financial conditions: "There is good money in it", or "it's a secure position", not to mention the cases of "your father was a ..., your grandfather was a...," so you will become a ...! Either way, tremendous amounts of people have found paying jobs and at times reached powerful positions with extensive decision-making authority. This has enormous consequences and can very well be the beginning of a long phase of personal and inner dissatisfaction causing the creation and circulation of negative energy with all its after-effects. Unfortunately, false decisions are often only questioned if connected with increasing failure or in extreme examples, lead to the onset of life-threatening diseases. We are familiar with the story of our ancestors who have worked a lifetime in one position or in one company or, at least, in a clearly limited field of activity in one profession. Even if that meant changing companies once in a while to take advantage of promotional prospects or when a company closed down on the other hand. Changing jobs very often though or even changing profession among the adults around us was by far more seldom than it is today. The job situation is changing rapidly though and to see this we just need to rethink the last three years of our personal career. If we haven't realized this by now, it could be due to the fact that most people tend to cling as long as possible to what they consider good or simply to what they know. Man has the distinctive desire to follow one thing as long as possible and stick to it, without challenging it, until life unmistakably tells us we are doing something wrong here. The human being is a creature of habit. We all know this in any coherence with ourselves. That's why we are better off working against our own comfort in conscious moments, providing information from different sources while listening and analyzing what we experience and listening to what our gut feeling says. Our guts are often our best advisors. That is why therapists and scientists also speak of the "gut-brain"!

Just because others are older than we are or because they have more money than we do, does not mean they have better concepts of life. It always pays to listen to what others have to say, however, we should form our own opinion on the basis of different experiences in different situations and with own experience.

We should plan our professional future as part of our lives based on what we really expect from life, as if we had already earned all the money in the world. If we recognize what we can give the world in our own very special way, with joy, without faking ourselves and what individual and universal experience and advantage could result from this, we'd suddenly be far removed from problems concerning job shortages, vacation planning, competitive thinking, social envy and retirement age. We could then finally begin to focus on our life as a whole.

## 02 | INTENTIONS AND CONTENTS OF THIS BOOK

This book supports us in finding a path for our life by giving us pointers for a long and happy life in harmony and personal freedom. It will open new perspectives and give us an approach to seeing life differently from the materially oriented and conventional work market. It is the manifested version of my knowledge gained through my practical experience in workshops, training sessions and other related jobs. It is meant to deepen, refresh or initiate discrete contemplation of the questions we ask ourselves at a time when are open for it. It is to be used in inner peace situations, the comfort of our home or away from the maybe unwanted, sometimes misleading or overwhelming group dynamic of a seminar or workshop.

"Follow your Calling" calls our individual qualities and needs directly to our consciousness to help us use our personal strengths genuinely and successfully, independent of current work market structures. We will become aware of our physical, mental and interpersonal potential and can create, based on our own individual values and goals, a picture of our "dream job". We will obtain a clear picture of our major strengths and transferable skills. At our own individual speed, we can work comfortably through our predestined fields of activity that best suit our skills. This book will help us find ways to an individually fitted, interesting purpose in life – regardless of what others may think – in which our qualities can be fully utilized and our needs optimally fulfilled. The goal is to find a job that feels like a "hobby", one in which we do exactly what we desire and we desire what we do.

Conventional institutions for job assistance, vocational retraining or further education courses limit themselves mainly to the current structure and try to "stuff" us into this framework, too.

Regardless of how modern the medium of information is, be it the unemployment office or services designed to find a job, this will be the case. Besides a few exceptions, we will only be offered jobs in the well-known, established or standardized professions. This doesn't necessarily help us any further. In the end it's only about finding what our commercial value is for others, the employers.

To be independent, besides having a certain amount of financial independency, you must have a definition of your own purpose and value. Basically, whoever has a clear vision, lives happier! Faith gives your life meaning. For many people by the way this begins in childhood with a religion of any kind.

The first step is the "clearing", the making up of ourselves so we can recognize the values and life circumstances that are personally important for us to find contentment. Through this, goals are created and to reach these goals, we need a plan. If you don't have a goal you will just become the target of other person's goals! In any case your life goals should be formulated concretely and manifested in writing; this will be helpful, now and later on.

Whoever works through this book diligently step-by-step will be rewarded with the following life advantages:

| A conscious and detailed picture of yourself
| Clarity on your individual qualities and needs
| A picture of your dream job and an approach to its realization
| Basic framework of your initial definition of fulfillment
| Creation of your life plan with goals and deadlines
| Improvement of your self-esteem and self-confidence
| Improvement of your personal social skills
| Confident perspectives on the educational and working world
| Mechanisms for effective education- and job hunting

# THIS BOOK IS A PERSONAL WORKBOOK TO BE KEPT AND TREASURED (IN YOUR OWN INTEREST)!

# 03 | SUGGESTED RULES FOR SUCCESSFUL USAGE

There are people (me being one of them) that sometimes need months or maybe even a year to finally finish a book. The result is, of course, unsatisfying because the contiguity is constantly being torn in fragments thus every time we must re-acclimate ourselves to the contents and never experience the suspense or the complete message. We are so busy with all the little imperfections of our intervening life that we cannot benefit from a book, which we bought for exactly this reason or which was given to us by well-meaning friends.

Sure, there are books that are more like music albums and serve mainly as entertainment to relax or perk us up. But because "Follow Your Calling" is a workbook, i.e. a book to actively work on ourselves and our best characteristics, the results will be congruent with the amount of importance, continuity and attention we give it – of what we give to ourselves! This applies to any other type of work: put a lot of energy into it and we get an abundance back, invest only a little, and we need not wonder about the modest results. This has to be clear from the beginning, otherwise we won't be working efficiently and that is an unnecessary waste of our energy!

I know, our daily routine doesn't always make it easy to follow these rules. But only when we – at least once – consequentially do more than the normal standard, we will be able to have an effect that will offer us more than our normal state. Many people don't make that clear to themselves or are just too comfortable the way they are. But to do more than the masses of people is the secret recipe of success. Once this step has been taken the amount of energy spent will seem minor in retrospect. This has to be done otherwise this is not going to work! If I do what the masses do, I get what the masses get: a mass product!

We should therefore set down some ground rules to consciously absorb our extracted knowledge and to use it to its full extent.

## THE FIRST RULE IS:

Work through this book in the shortest time possible! Don't let it lie around and act as if other things are more important. Finish this task first until you are sure of what you think and do. Only when you have the complete picture are you allowed to talk about it. Otherwise there is a danger of others talking us out of our good ideas before they have completely matured.

## THE SECOND RULE IS:

Always seek out a quiet spot to read and write your spontaneous ideas down immediately, if possible in detail, before you start second guessing yourself and distort them. Write them down as they flow from your mind, your "guts" or your heart. Some people make fun of others who make decisions based on their "gut feeling" or their "heart". In true fact the largest amount of nerves found outside the brain are in the region of the heart and digestive system, in particular, the intestinal region that is predominantly found in the stomach. So it is absolutely no coincidence when we make decisions based on our "gut feeling". I have even made extra space for this topic in the book. If you need more space, use the empty pages at the end of the book or take an extra piece of paper. Some people can write a lot in a few words, others need more words to picture their thoughts.

In the beginning and in the breaks of my workshops I play a short song, a fanfare, to help with relaxation and concentration so that the participants can easily find their way back to focusing again. In Tai Chi, we bow shortly before every class and leave our daily problems behind us. Perhaps you can create your own little ritual to give yourself the attention you need when you occupy yourself with this book? Once we have begun, only the "here and now" is valid. We are talking about perhaps 30 hours of our life and it will not progress any further if we deal with problems of the past or fears of the future. That would be a complete waste of energy! Our work in this book will deliver an approach to solutions regarding questions we have long contemplated. Even when we perhaps at first think that it applies to other areas. That is why it is important to be open and attentive to the contents and to "listen closely". I always remember a saying that I myself learned from a workshop leader that has always stuck with me: "Be here and live in the moment!" He was right because there was always a danger of me (and others) getting hung up on details, digressing in my thoughts and not concentrating on the present.

## FURTHER RULES ARE:

Be honest with yourself! There's only one person you can cheat when you are dealing with self-enlightenment. That's right, you yourself! This is perhaps the decisive advantage of a book over a workshop, seminar or other type of outside therapy. We don't have to prove ourselves to anyone, except ourselves, and later as a side effect, those who love us and whom we love. Otherwise no one! What we gain from this book (and naturally from any other activity) depends completely on how open and intensively we participate. Therefore only one motto can apply here: be unprejudiced, be spontaneous. Go with your spontaneous gut feeling when working through this book and all its exercises. The results will be substantially better if we stick to the ground rules and deal with the material openly. A defensive attitude will just block our cognitive ability to deal with the contents. Another danger of wasting your valuable energy!

Be courageous in your ideas and fantasies, even be a little overzealous, but not too far-fetched from reality. Be comfortable with the goals you set yourself.

I am an author, not a judge and this book (as a medium) is not here to judge or prejudge. I am not grading you on this for I am, myself, not perfect (yuk, how boring). The book does not want to "command" anyone even when some of the readers may feel this way temporarily because when genuinely confronted with themselves, they are not always initially comfortable with the attained results. The book is the catalyst, the substance that induces and expedites reactions. The mirror that helps us to find answers to the questions: "Who am I?" and "What do I – really – want?" In other words, our external conscience, the angel and the devil in one person! The critical part that we cannot provide voluntarily because we normally switch off to our comfort zone when confronted with these questions, sometimes from fear of another suspected truth?

I know it is generally well accepted that during a task you can occupy yourself with another or perhaps many tasks at the same time. I am advising you that during your work through this book (and optimally during your breaks) you should abstain from the following: I-pod, cell phone, telephone calls, parties and drugs of any sort (unless prescribed by your doctor). Preferably also no sex, no TV, no newspapers/magazines, no verbal conversations (or only what is required) with parents, friends, siblings or other partners. Whoever wants to work diligently through this book in "one piece" and achieve the most success, will advise and ask their family and friends in advance for their cooperation. The motto is "Living in Silence"! In this manner you can intensify the conversation with yourself. "Only still waters reflect a clear mirror image." Everything else is only a distraction. Even when listening to your I-pod or whatever, you are no longer alone in your self-dialogue.

Whoever is subconsciously eagerly awaiting a text message on their cell phone can never be completely immersed in themselves. The experimental goal here is to contemplate on myself, and my future. A good opportunity for this is the weekend, a trip, or holidays and vacation in general because during these periods we are generally more open-minded. I was employed in distribution for many years and have driven long stretches. Those were the times I could contemplate freely, since I was highly concentrated anyway – but don't read while driving!

Don't try to do the second or third part before doing the first! Read the book from front to back and top to bottom. Even when the substance doesn't seem to apply to you, it is still a part of the total insight you gain. We will spoil the results when we go directly to the summary of all the previous exercises. Details will be lost along the way and valuable insight can be lost!

Details of the contents and methods in this book are only defined for us. If you liked the book and should come into conversation about it, recommend it to your friends but be sure not to divulge any details. That would be unfair! Future readers would possibly miss that "Aha effect" by wanting to take the third step without making the first thereby impairing their personal success. The same goes for conversation with persons who have already worked through the book. Don't let others "bend your ears" with their results before you are completely finished. There's a danger of you becoming timid and you will only block yourself!

The book can only serve its purpose for you since your notes in the book won't really help someone else; they would only be a distraction and falsify the individual results.

Any feedback worth mentioning for the improvement in quality of future editions of this, other books, and the respective workshop topics, is naturally welcome. Even problems that you thought were unique can be of use to future participants. We are never alone with our problems. There is always someone, somewhere who has the same or very similar problem; one you thought was yours alone.

Suggestions, questions or comments on the book can be submitted gladly to the author. He will try to contact you within the framework of his other activities. For this purpose, please use the email address found under *www.rare-ware.info*.

AFTER THESE FORMALITIES AND ADVICE WE NOW COME TO THE ACTIVE PART OF THE BOOK. VOILA!

# 04 | MY CHARACTERISTICS "WHO AM I TODAY?"

Before we follow the road in the direction of our true calling, we will need to take an inventory or determine our position. In this manner we can gain a clear picture of where we currently stand – and why? In the long run this will be conducive to our orientation and security.

What we are doing here is certainly the first experience for some in specific conscious deliberation of their own personality. Of course, everyone broods at one time, maybe even often, about life. But many of these attempts and approaches are thwarted when we are up against our inner resistance; when our weaknesses appear and we don't really like what we see once we have thought it over exactly. Without a critical authority accompanying us we end up in a circle that never moves into the depths but instead leaves us feeling comfortable on a superficial level. You tell yourself: just don't cause turmoil in your mind or take an accurate look at yourself. We could find out some uncomfortable truths about ourselves as soon as we start poking around in our life. This is the attitude the majority of mankind takes. They don't realize that the truth will catch up with them eventually and they will no longer be able to regulate their life through their complacency.

It is worth it, in any case, to immediately tackle and rectify recognized problems or discrepancies of your own personality and lifestyle. Repressed problems will only grow larger, not smaller. Some people run, as a last resort, to psychologists, therapists, churchgoers or other advisors because they are promised more competence. Actually, we can be our own best adviser and other sought-out advisors often don't do much more than asking questions, only to tell us what we actually knew about ourselves all along. We just haven't accepted ourselves as our own authority or haven't demanded enough of ourselves. This leads back to the fact that we have never consciously concerned ourselves with going to the depths of our personality; to manifest this insight and have it available for less euphoric times. We are going to change all this now!

We will fall back on acquired knowledge of ourselves, which we have cheerfully and from our own initiative, bravely and voluntarily compiled with foresight. "Follow your Calling" is a recipe book. At first we will follow the given instructions and make a standard dish. With more routine and experience, we can adapt that recipe to fit our needs by spicing it up.

Our first active step is to now create a "Calling Card". I like to call it a "testimonial" because we bear testimony to ourselves at a specific point in time. We make a basic statement about our life today, a snapshot of this point in time! This is true now. A prerequisite for all the exercises in this book are always spontaneity, honesty and positive thinking!

Please answer all the following questions completely and explicitly according to this principle: I have to decide on one thing.

"IT BEGINS WITH YOUR DESIRED AGE AND FAVORITE COLOR. I AM GOING ON BOARD AND AM ALLOWED ONLY ONE ITEM THAT I MUST TAKE WITH ME. NOTHING MORE, NOTHING LESS."

MY NAME IS ...............................................................................................................................................

I AM ..........YEARS OF AGE. I WOULD LIKE TO LIVE TO ......... YEARS OF AGE.

DATE / PLACE / TIME NOW ...........................................................................................................

I AM CURRENTLY DOING
(FAMILY / FRIENDS / JOB / SCHOOL / HOBBIES / INTERESTS):

.......................................................................................................................................................

.......................................................................................................................................................

.......................................................................................................................................................

.......................................................................................................................................................

MY FAVORITE COLOR IS .............................................................................................................

MY DREAM IS

.......................................................................................................................................................

.......................................................................................................................................................

.......................................................................................................................................................

.......................................................................................................................................................

.......................................................................................................................................................

I COMPLETELY DISLIKE

.......................................................................................................................................................

.......................................................................................................................................................

.......................................................................................................................................................

.......................................................................................................................................................

.......................................................................................................................................................

Have you answered all the questions to all the themes listed? Were you spontaneous, honest and generous with yourself? Did you write the date down? It allows you to supervise yourself discipline in your approach to the book and the advice for continuity of the third chapter! It's also good for later reconstruction of the phases of our personal development.

Whoever doesn't have enough space on the given pages can simply take more paper. One of our goals should be to express ourselves straightforwardly. For many issues we need only a few words to describe ourselves precisely. This trains the mind; makes internal and external relationships clearer i.e., for us and for others. We detangle ourselves slowly, but surely, saving energy for more important issues.

By filling out the previous page we have at any rate clearly stated our position on at least five decisive themes of our life. This is a good starting position because we have at the same time created a timeframe in which we can for example, – based on our current knowledge – realize at least one of our dreams. Besides that, we have called a few "ingredients" and circumstances of our life into consciousness, which allows them to be readily accessible. We will have more opportunities to do this in the following chapters.

# 05 | GUIDED FANTASY: REVIEWING MY LIFE

Throughout the entire book, we will be dealing with the "clarification" of our true personality and the resulting higher self-consciousness and self-confidence which provides us with support to develop a very own, vested feeling of self esteem with which we can better concentrate on our expectations in life. We first now need to create clarity and strength from our past to create a good basis for this higher self-consciousness and self-confidence.

Because we have been alive for a good amount of time now, we have developed many talents, skills, qualities and needs through plenty of experience that have secured or improved our "survival" in general. In addition to this, we carry in our genes not only the directly inherited genetic information from our relatives, but also the complete wisdom of the historic development of mankind until to date, in general. So we are actually very well taken care of and sufficiently prepared. The problem for most people though, is to localize these wells of knowledge and to be able to tap from them for their own use. We want to therefore once – in retrospect – observe ourselves to realize why we are or have become what we are. What has led us to be the person we now portray? We could also use the term "introspection" or self-observation (observation of our experiences); a phenomenon of communication within ourselves to reach individual enlightenment. We will, of course, document this in writing to have this treasure available at a later time.

That being said, we will begin our journey into our past! Some call it the "guided dream trip" or the "guided fantasy"; in any case the effect is, at best, the same. We will let ourselves go and head to a place where we would like to reflect on ourselves and our lives.

Take your writing material with you for documentation of your most significant impressions to keep them spontaneous and original.

Singles usually won't have a problem finding a quiet spot in their apartment but if you have a roommate, be sure to seek out as undisturbed a spot as possible. That can be a park bench, the relaxation room at the gym or someplace outside the direct line of traffic. Because this is about the dialog within you, distractions such as music, cell phones prepared for sensation, or loud public places will only divert us from this task. In a properly guided meditation where others give us their thought impulses, a little light background music can help you relax but if you want to read and retain, do it in silence. Like the old Asian saying goes (the Buddha): "ONLY STILL WATERS REFLECT A CLEAR MIRROR IMAGE." That is exactly what we want to retain here!

To be able to relax, I suggest you breathe in deeply and hold your breath shortly to review your recent stress situation. Then exhale and at the same time let go of all the stress that has stolen your creative energy. Breathe in deeply once again and tense up your total body, starting with your butt to the tips of your toes and then the stomach, up into the shoulders to your face and arms; then breathe out and release with it the total tenseness from your body that was making you stiff. No matter what has transpired in the last half an hour, no matter what will happen in the next hour. It's not worth wasting energy on that; for now we are reading and we need not worry about anything else but what is right in front of us.

The following text is part of a guided meditation. In this case we have to guide ourselves. Maybe we have an empathetic friend who can read the following text slowly and clearly. In which case light, relaxing music can be played but if you're not sure this will work for you,

then read it yourself, if possible in one piece until page 39.
IT WILL GET INTENSE!

We continue breathing evenly and already we find ourselves in thought; someplace on an adventure out in nature, far away from the city with its noise, smells, hectic and other restrictions. In a peaceful gentle climate with pleasant scents and colorful changing backgrounds we come slowly to a smaller path that gradually becomes overgrown with thicket until it leads us to a warm, pretty and pleasant-smelling field of flowers. The sun is shining, the birds are chirping, as we pleasurably lie in the soft grass and look aimlessly into the beautiful blue skies so we can ponder about ourselves in peace.

Now that we are lying here so peacefully, it's really easy to let our life pass over us consciously with detachment and peace. We don't want to be aggravated or judge incidents that date back several years. We only want to reflect soberly: what actually happened and when? How and why did certain circumstances in our lives develop?

For this, we will go way back to the year we were born and consider the month, season and time of day we were born. Do you really know about this? Have you ever given any thought to the time of day and the circumstances under which you were born? Have you ever discussed this with your parents or other important figures in your life? Are there any documents or mementos that will make us shrewder? Write the facts down, they are essential figures for your life!

Since when do we actually have our first name/s and do we like them? Do we like our family name? Why did our parents give us this name and who or what was the determining character or event? What role does our name play in our life? Has it influenced us in any way? What does it say about our personality? Where did we live or where do we consider our place of birth? Where, do you think, are your personal roots? What feelings do we have in conjunction with our name and our first accommodation? WRITE THEM DOWN!

How old and in what personal situation were your parents at your time of birth? If we don't know our birth parents we will be interested in our first conscious experience with our psychological parents or another significant person(s) in our life. Were they well-off, not only materially but spiritually? What did they look like back then; what kind of clothing, what type of style and which social standards ruled then? Who were their friends? Which friends, which dreams and which fears or worries could they have had back then? Would they perhaps have similar problems or enjoy themselves as we do today? In reality, how did your parents get along back then in their profession and in private? What recollections or perceptions do you have of this time? WRITE THEM DOWN!

Now we see ourselves as babies. We see our baby bed, our crib or even our bassinet! Our room, our toys, our home! What can we remember from this earlier time? Do we have any recollection of the space that was our small world? Any distinctive impressions of our first experiences that have shaped us? What feelings do we awaken when we look back on our early childhood?

We are becoming older and bigger, and now we are a small child. Perhaps we spend our time with a "nanny" or go to a kindergarten? Who are our most significant reference persons at this time? Can you remember names or faces? How much time do we spend with our parents, siblings, grandparents or other relatives, acquaintances or earlier playmates? Whom and what do we remember the most intensely in this respect and why? Who are our first friends, or with whom did we play with – then? Which were our favorite dolls or cuddly toys and can we remember their names and what they meant for us? WRITE THEM DOWN!

Today is the first day of school with our new satchel that we now see clearly and proudly in front of us. A new slice of life with new responsibilities begins! What year was that exactly? What was the name of our teacher then? Do we see our classroom or other pictures of our school in our mind? What was the social situation like back then? Was there anything special about our environment? What was the time like in school, such as the recesses, handicrafts and what was it like learning to read, write and do math? What could we do particularly well? What was our favorite subject? Did we take a class trip? If so, how did we feel when we were there? With whom and with what did we spend most of our time with? Do we still have contact with these persons or why and when did the contact break off? What can we remember about this time now? WRITE IT DOWN!

What role did our parents play during these first years of school; what did we experience with them? How did we normally spend our days? How often were our parents there for us, a little or a lot? Who had the most time for us? If and where did we go on vacation? What did we experience there? What can we remember exactly although it was perhaps only a "small" incident? What typical characteristics of our parents do we remember from this time? What was of particular importance to them – for us – and life in general? Which themes were issues of communication between us? What can we remember vividly? WRITE IT DOWN!

First it was elementary school, then middle school, high school, college, university or another type of schooling. What year was that again? How do we feel about these continuing school years in retrospect? Did everything run smoothly or was there a time when we particularly slipped up? What did we learn through this? What were our favorite subjects in our later years of school and exactly why were these our favorite subjects? Did we graduate from our aspired level of schooling and how did we feel afterwards? Did we almost drop out before the official end of our schooling? What was the reason for this? Which were the most uncomfortable memories and which the most pleasant?

What was our first romance like, the exciting parties, flirts, class trips, school outings and other events? How has our position in society developed in total? How have we changed, personally? How did our relationships develop with our parents, siblings and grandparents? Who was our best friend at this time? Do we still have contact with him or her? If yes, what connects us and when did we realize it? If no, why did we go separate ways? WRITE IT DOWN!

Depending on our current age, we have lived and are living through further stages and stations of our personal and professional development that can be (or have been) very individual and diverse. Of special importance for the personality and our acquired talents and skills are, however, these preceding first, and hopefully "careless" years of our life. They play a dominant role in our inherent lifestyle in later years.

Over the course of our lives we have lived through different stages that don't necessarily coincide with the development stages of a baby to school graduate, worker, employee or other professional "adults", respectively. Where would we place ourselves in these diverse phases of our life? Would you say that you have gone through each of these conventional stages or have you developed your own individual stages?

Did we relocate at anytime? When did we travel for the first time without our parents? Where did we go and with whom? What was so special about it? When did we discover our gender, I mean the realization of "I am a girl" (woman) or "I am a boy" (man). How do we relate to this realization? What does this realization have to do with our security, our personal maturity self-fulfillment and personal freedom? When was the first time we perceived our first erotic experience? When did we have our first boy or girlfriend? What attracted us to each other? When did we have sex for the first time? When was the first time we consciously enjoyed sex? What experiences have we made in this essential area of becoming an adult? WRITE IT DOWN!

When was the first time in our lives that we ever experienced a competitive situation, incident or comparison in performance? When did we meet resistance for the first time on important issues? When did we make the first concrete decision regarding our daily lives? How resolute were we about it? When did we land our first paying job (also part-time)? What were the reasons for this job? How did we feel about it? WRITE IT DOWN!

How do we actually feel about our acceptance in society presently i.e., our family, circle of friends, school, or amongst work colleagues? How do we deal with our age? Do we feel good? How much energy do we have in comparison to phases of the past? Have we actually experienced a great deal or too little? In which phase do we see our personal life career ladder, both professionally and personally? WRITE IT DOWN!

Have we ever experienced a real need for material goods or food? Have we ever been in need of psychological help i.e., had emotional problems that no one seemed able to help us with? If yes, when exactly was this and what caused this? Have these problems since then been resolved or are there presently conflict situations of this type? WRITE IT DOWN!

Who were or are our mentors or role models and for what reason? Which of their achievements or events are commendable to us i.e., which methods and ideals are worth striving for or imitating? Which word, slogan or virtue could best describe our general concept of ethics and morals, based on our own general moral values and behavior? WRITE IT DOWN!

Whom or what do we definitely not want in our life and what would we immediately dispose of if we had the power to something good? What would we immediately implement if we had the power to do so? What (positive) role do we play in society? Do we have any idea? If "yes", WRITE DOWN IMMEDIATELY!

Where do we generally seek out our information; from what sources do we draw our knowledge? Are they always first-hand sources, or possibly second or third-hand sources that, in turn, obtain their information from yet other sources? Do we question these sources? Are the media and methods with which we inform ourselves truly competent and effective? Are there perhaps basic valid questions to which we already have an answer (if someone should ask us)? Things we think we could do better than the ones doing them now although we have not yet actively addressed the material or have not had a chance to show our competence? Which things are these? WRITE THEM DOWN, FAST!

What can we actually do very well, even though we haven't necessarily had proper training in this field? Which skills are these? How and where did we learn them? For what reason? Do we actually use this potential? To date, what has turned out to be the best method for learning and assimilating information for us? WRITE IT DOWN!

In what stage of life do we see ourselves? Are there sectors of our life where our experiences are perhaps much more advanced than "normal", even if we do not see any "commercial value" in them at this time? Which sectors are these and if we were to consider our "life's work": what is or could be our lifework even if we think we haven't made a conscious step in this direction yet or haven't had any success at doing so? WRITE IT DOWN!

How would we rate our degree of fulfillment regarding our lifework or purpose in life on a scale of 0 to 100? Are we at the beginning, in the middle, or very advanced? When will our lifework be completed? When do we have reached our goal in life? Objectives? Ideas? Dreams? Write them down immediately as "phantastic" as they may seem! AFTER THAT, RELAX!

We are still lying in that field of beautiful flowers, observing ourselves today and realize that it is not at all worth wasting energy on the negative incidents of our past. They are, though, an integral part of our life's experiences and along with the positive experiences made during this time they have allowed us to grow personally in a very special way. And so we have now either found or sketched answers, or at least an approach, to many questions of our lives that we will, after further investigation, crystallize with the help of this book. We see ourselves again as a complete being, one who is what he/she is, with a past that we nonetheless have to accept. Even if we believe that we have had an exceptionally hard and joyless life; in the end we have survived and can immediately begin to do things differently for we at least know for sure what we don't want. We will simply strip those negative experiences off like a veil, and begin to concentrate on the best experiences of our past and a better future that we will now actively and consciously shape. Accompanying us will be an unbelievably massive power that no one can take from us: the power to take an individually chosen standpoint with a positive outlook on the future!

In this connection, it will also be of interest to reflect on what we have felt during this trip through our past. Did we have many or few connecting "films" that played before our eyes? Did we have gaps in particular timeframes or especially intensive phases of recollection? At exactly which point(s) did we feel inner resistance to the questions we asked ourselves precisely so we could obtain true insight? We should record these points for now or highlight them in our notes so we can follow up more intensively at a later point. Perhaps we will be more open or have won further insight that will allow us a deeper approach in this area?

For our complete comprehension it is, however, important to grasp that we have just provided a decisive component for further insight into the conscious knowledge of our personality even when the individual has drawn more or less "new" or unknown knowledge until now, into consciousness. The results are as individual as the human being in general.

Many may have felt while reflecting intensively: oh my God, there's so much surfacing, how in the world can I write it down so quickly? Others have felt resistance when thinking explicitly in some individual areas while others yet have only had short spurts of thoughts and couldn't get closer to the substance? It doesn't matter; we're only on page 39!

In any case, we have created a revitalized, "rounded" picture of ourselves. We are not reading a novel here or a fairy tale, but rather observing the exciting factual report on our life that will become the foundation for the (more) successful handling of our life from here on. Combined with the liberated present, only a self-honest, accepting and – in part – forgiving, relationship to situations and people of our past or present will enable us to focus unbiased on valuable perspectives of our future. We can do this without any further waste of our energy regarding the past, for we have now made our peace with it. We have entered and filed what has happened under "experience" for the sake of our future.

This chapter has been the first step in this direction. In the following chapters we will draw on a few positive, formative details of our past so we can then concentrate on the present and how we can possibly use these for opportunities in the future. We will become the managers of our life, pursuing "Life Management" i.e., wise management of our lives, like a good manager leads his firm to a long and success business life.

# 06 | MY INDIVIDUAL QUALITIES

Every human being can do something special in his own unique manner, which is an inimitable part of our personality. Every person develops his own very individual and one-of-a-kind qualities, talents and skills in the course of their lives. Even if we are not aware of them, they are our "icing on the cake" based on all general human qualities from which we all somewhere during our lives have received our share and yet the characteristics vary from person to person. They are the evidence and the guarantee not only for our ability to survive but for our quality of life!

Through progressing genetic research I am absolutely sure we will learn that many more of these essential, influential "conditions" have already been predetermined in our genes. In spite of this, the final distinction and evolution takes place during the formative and empirical course of life, especially in the first twenty years.

In this chapter we will be dealing with our entirely individual qualities, which I have divided into the following two categories

1 | Our more "emotional" qualities. I have named them this because we have developed these, so to speak, on the wayside during our lives. Qualities we have adapted from our social environment in our dealings with other human beings of a particular society. Independently and without pressure to perform; mainly free from financial interest or competition.

2 | Our more "rational" qualities. I call them this because they hold a portion of commercial viability within them; because their value can be gauged and in part contain a comparatively competitive nature.

We will be able to determine the differences by comparing these two terms in the following schemes. Important for our work on these charts are the following rules:

We will choose the qualities that fit us best; those that can be attributed to us – from our viewpoint – even if we haven't yet openly shown them in public. At the same time be generous but honest with yourselves. We are not accountable to anyone except ourselves. Of importance is to observe if we spontaneously sense any of these listed qualities in us. Don't think about it for too long, otherwise your self-doubt can easily destroy your intuition!

As soon as we have read one of the terms and understand it, we receive an inner impulse that either says: "No, that's not me!" or "Yes, that's me!" All spontaneous "Yes" answers are to be quickly circled – no matter how many there are! Should we have the feeling that we didn't completely understand the meaning of a term, we can always look it up in the dictionary, but we usually have spontaneous intuition for what each term means.

The provided charts are just an example of terms that have proven practical over the course of time. Some terms may overlap with others, but that doesn't matter! This is due to the fact that different people prefer one terminology over the other. What is important is the spontaneity of your decision!

If you feel you have special qualities not mentioned here then just write them in the space allotted at the bottom of the page. Any questions? No? Good! Now, let's see how many hidden qualities are stored inside you. HAVE FUN!

# MY MORE EMOTIONAL QUALITIES

YES, I AM ...

| | | | |
|---|---|---|---|
| BALANCED | STABLE | SPIRITUAL | WILLFUL |
| ACCEPTING | FAITHFUL | BRAVE | PROTECTIVE |
| CARING | UNDERSTANDING | GENEROUS | PATIENT |
| SENSITIVE | COMPASSIONATE | INQUISITIVE | CONSIDERATE |
| IMPULSIVE | FORGIVING | SINCERE | LOVING |
| REALISTIC | CREATIVE | IMAGINATIVE | VISIONARY |
| SPONTANEOUS | HONEST | HARMONIOUS | NATURAL |
| MUSICAL | PLAYFUL | AGILE | ROMANTIC |
| CONFIDENT | INTUITIVE | RELAXED | LIVELY |
| KNOWLEDGEABLE | HELPFUL | EXTRAORDINARY | HUMOROUS |
| CURIOUS | TALKATIVE | CAREFUL | POWERFUL |
| HAPPY | CHARMING | GENTLE | UNIQUE |

# MY MORE RATIONAL QUALITIES

YES, I AM ...

| | | | |
|---|---|---|---|
| ADAPTABLE | MOTIVATED | PERSEVERING | ENTHUSIASTIC |
| PERSISTENT | PRUDENT | ORGANIZED | DIPLOMATIC |
| DISCREET | ASSERTIVE | ANALYTICAL | EFFECTIVE |
| DECISIVE | FLEXIBLE | ACCURATE | EFFICIENT |
| INNOVATIVE | COMPETENT | OUTGOING | COOPERATIVE |
| FRUGAL | CULTIVATED | PERFORMANCE-ORIENTED | ADAPTIVE |
| LOYAL | METHODICAL | TEAM-ORIENTED | PUNCTUAL |
| PROFICIENT | FAST-WORKING | INDEPENDENT | REASONABLE |
| THOROUGH | TACTFUL | DELIBERATE | TIRELESS |
| RESPONSIBLE | RELIABLE | DIVERSE | PROSPECTIVE |
| LOGICAL | OPEN-MINDED | PRACTICAL | ENERGETIC |
| COMMITTED | RATIONAL | POLITE | FAIR |

Did you circle all your "secret" qualities? Were you courageous and honest with yourself? Did you strike through qualities that had possibly been circled in euphoria until our courage left us and we downsized ourselves because others perhaps don't see us this way? Make sure you keep those on the list. Check yourself again: "Who am I?" We are allowed to circle anything that could possibly apply to us in any form. The book's not going to bite us for that because we are here interviewing ourselves!

So, if we're sure we have done everything correctly we will leave this exercise with a good "gut feeling". So, just do it. We will return to these pages later! This was not just a happy circling game to allow ourselves a few jolly moments. We will continue to work on this later and delve deeper but for now we want to take a look at some other areas. Therefore we will first engage ourselves with further areas of our personality in relation to our calling; what we really should do to be happy in the long run.

By the way, you should have at least circled one specific word from both of the previous charts. Otherwise I will have to coach you on how to have faith in yourself! Have a quick look once again to make sure you understood the exercise: what did he write again at the beginning of the chapter? That's right: UNIQUE!

This fact is for many of us not obvious or even embarrassing. Many people do not feel this way and so it will be even more difficult to get these people to accept the fact that they are just as unique as anyone else. Simply try to believe it.

Those who cannot believe it, give up a significant piece of their personal freedom. The more aware you become of this fact, the more secure you will become with yourself and your uniqueness! In case you haven't done it, then circle it now resolutely while letting the word "Unique" melt in your mouth and simply feel good about it! We're now moving on to the next important field of our personality.

# 07 | MY INDIVIDUAL NEEDS

To be able to make full use of the individual qualities, our individual needs have to be satisfied. If we want to be a successful driver at the Formula One auto races, it will do us no good to arrive with a tractor even if we're the best driver in the world. There are basic conditions that must be fulfilled to reach a halfway satisfying result. We need to have a vehicle that is suitable for the Formula One race. What we then make out of it and how well it functions is a mixture of practice, talent and tweaking of various technical details; not to mention luck. Sure, we can make the best out of a situation – some people are experts at this when I look at their positions – but we will never be able to completely achieve or experience what is truly feasible if the basic conditions are not there.

This has nothing to do with material needs. We will observe that it is often completely different needs that serve the basis for a satisfying life. Material satisfaction almost always follows as an automatic factor derived from holistic contentment of the body, mind and soul. An extreme desire and display of material goods indicate a deprived state of spiritual and emotional yearning.

In the next chart and in the same manner as before, we will circle our needs that must be filled to enhance and use our qualities to their full extent so we can feel absolute contentment. We will be asking ourselves: What needs must be met to ensure this is a situation where I can develop and experience long-term happiness? Please answer with self-confidence and start circling spontaneously, as before!

# MY INDIVIDUAL NEEDS

YES, I NEED ...

| | | | |
|---|---|---|---|
| LOVE | WISDOM | FUN | HARMONY |
| FAITH | CONFIRMATION | HONESTY | FANTASY |
| HEALTH | BEAUTY | EVEN-TEMPEREDNESS | TRUST |
| JUSTICE | PATIENCE | LOYALTY | SPONTANEITY |
| OBLIGATION | INTEGRATION | POWER | SUSPENSE |
| HUMOR | CREATIVITY | PROTECTION | FREEDOM |
| COMPANIONSHIP | GUIDANCE | UNDERSTANDING | PEACE |
| FAMILY | INTIMACY | RESPONSIBILITY | SENSITIVITY |
| EXCLUSIVENESS | NATURALNESS | CORDIALITY | WARMTH |
| LIGHT | KNOWLEDGE | FERTILITY | ORGANIZATION |
| STABILITY | ADMIRATION | ENERGY | GENEROSITY |
| EROTICISM | DISCIPLINE | ROMANTICISM | SILENCE |
| ................... | ................... | ................... | ................... |

Here again the principle of being honest with ourselves applies, but this time also the principle of modesty. Please don't play the role of the touchy princess and the pea, the frustrated diva or mother's favorite and in frustration circle everything we believe we need for quick self-satisfaction, just to have it. Think about it carefully: what do I really need to be happy?

It is not about acquiring material possessions so that we can even begin to show interest, direction or achievement. That has to be clear to ourselves first because no one cares if we are in the midst of self-realization. Especially not if we are working for others and act as assistants in helping them fulfilling their life concepts through our support. No, it is about finding out what we believe our optimal environment should look like. In other words, the goal of our development. For what attainable situation is it worth working for? Where and for which goal are we willing to apply our talent(s)?

If we can imagine precisely what our ideal target area should look like, we attain a further factor to more clarity, direction and, naturally, the motivation to pursue it. We then have something we can believe in and that is the first step to achieving our goal. Some people already do achieve a completely satisfactory situation in their current jobs and in other social fields. Purely because they have not only thought about what they don't want but about what they want and are therefore clear and free in their heads!

After all our courageous, spontaneous and honest answering of the previous questions, we leave this chapter behind us and reach the last hurdle of our personality analysis through the coach that knows us the best (have you had a look in the mirror today?) Now it is about gathering concrete information.

# 08 | MY INDIVIDUAL SKILLS

Like in the earlier chapters of this book there follows another round of circling answers. We want to get as close as possible to ourselves. That's why we are now going to delve into three different areas of our individual skills and interests. Besides our pure human qualities and needs, we have gained throughout our lives further knowledge, talents and skills which we are perhaps not conscious of. For some re- ason at one point in our life we may have decided that they weren't important and repressed them? It could be that, in fact, some of the expertise we possess was already pronounced in childhood in a phase where it was treated more as fun-oriented than "rational". Eventually, we thought of these experiences as unimportant or cir- cumstantial because others we considered to be important leaders or role models perhaps told us to "forget it" or "that's not you". Even perhaps because they themselves may had had negative experien- ces in similar situations? Or we sensed the skills in ourselves but didn't know what to do with it, where to use it, or doubted it was of any good or importance?

We have three further charts regarding these themes:
a | MATERIALS OR THINGS
b | INFORMATION OR
c | PEOPLE

Basically, we are moving along using the same principles, namely courage and effortless self-honestly as beforehand. When we don't see the items we are looking for, simply add them to the list. However, the themes differ somewhat and I will explain the procedure for every theme separately in advance.

a | MATERIALS OR THINGS
Look through the list of items/concepts and choose the ones that appeal to you in any kind of form – even ones you have no experience with or dealt with actively or consciously. If in doubt, pick those that spontaneously appeal to you, things you take pleasure in doing, something that appeals to your talents or makes you happy. If we have had any dealings in these fields and our decisions are based on experience, even better!

b | INFORMATION
This is about how we best assimilate information and knowledge, in other words how we want to gain, absorb or relay that information to others. It doesn't matter if we have done this before or not! What appeals to us spontaneously? Please address the terms exactly and distinguish between the subtle differences. Especially the last twelve information types are in their declaration somewhat unusual but you will have some association with it. Information as a "Solution to Problems" means for example:

In essence, the reality that a problem has been solved, but no statement has been made regarding the method or accuracy. Here we have to try to evaluate only the core of the message, without long interpretation by picking out the phrases that are logical to you. One always makes some sort of association when reading these phrases, intuitively.

c | PEOPLE

What type of people mainly interests us? This doesn't necessarily mean we should spend our entire (private) lives with these people! (If we work for someone, we work with them). In all three charts, be brave enough to circle everything that appeals to you!

# MATERIALS OR THINGS

YES, THIS APPEALS TO ME ...

| | | | |
|---|---|---|---|
| PAPER | NUMBERS | WOOD | METAL |
| INVESTMENTS | PLASTICS | FABRICS | LEATHER |
| WATER | EARTH | PLANTS | CHEMICALS |
| MACHINES | TOOLS | TOYS | EQUIPMENT |
| MONEY | FURNITURE | COMPUTERS | PAINTS |
| CONSTRUCTION MATERIALS | CLOTHES | HOUSEHOLD ARTICLES | HOME TEXTILES |
| JEWELRY | ANTIQUES | HOUSEHOLD APPLIANCES | COSMETICS |
| MEDICINE | ELECTRICITY | ANIMALS | FOODS |
| PLANT-DERIVED PRODUCTS | ENERGY | SHOES | ELECTRONICS |
| ELECTRONIC COMPONENTS | AUDIO MEDIA | VISUAL MEDIA | PRINT MEDIA |
| ENTERTAINMENT MEDIA | MUSICAL INSTRUMENTS | TELECOMMUNI- CATION | INFORMATION MEDIA |
| TEACHING AIDS/DEVICES | SPORTING GOODS | PEOPLE | TRANSPORTATION |

# INFORMATION

YES, I ASSIMILATE INFORMATION THROUGH THE FOLLOWING MEDIA ...

| | | | |
|---|---|---|---|
| BOOKS | MAGAZINES | NEWSPAPERS | CATALOGS |
| INSTRUCTION MANUALS | RECORDS | LITERATURE | VIDEO INFORMATION |
| AUDIO INFORMATION | COMPUTER PRINTOUTS | LIVE SEMINARS | LIVE WORKSHOPS |
| GUIDED COURSES | STATISTICS | REPORTS | STUDIES |
| SURVEY | FACTS AND FIGURES | HISTORICAL DATA | SYMBOLS |
| RESEARCH | OPINION RESEARCH | OVERVIEWS | MANUALS |
| FUNDAMENTALS | MATERIALS (SAMPLES) | INTELLECTUAL (EXAMPLES) | BASIS (CORE VALUE) |
| STANDARDS | ORGANIZATIONS | SYSTEMS | PROGRAMS |
| METHODS | TECHNIQUES | PROCEDURES | ANALYSIS |
| PRINCIPLES OF APPLICATION | PRACTICAL RECOMMENDATIONS | POLITICAL | PROJECT OBJECTIVES |
| OBJECTIVITY TO THEME/S... | SOLUTIONS TO PROBLEMS... | APPROXIMATION OF TRUTH… | PROJECT PLANNING |
| TACTICAL IMPORTANCE OF... | COMPETENCE TO... | DEBILITATION OF ... | CONTROL OVER... |

# PEOPLE

YES, THESE TYPES OF PEOPLE INTEREST ME ...

| MALE | FEMALE | BOTH (M+F) | ALL AGE GROUPS |
|---|---|---|---|
| ADOLESCENTS | STUDENTS | YOUNG ADULTS (20-30 YRS OF AGE) | "MID-THIRTIES" (30-40 YRS OF AGE) |
| "MIDDLEAGED" (40-50 YRS. OF AGE) | LATE MIDDLE AGE (BEGINNING AT 50) | RETIREES/ PENSIONERS | EVERYONE REGARDLESS OF SEXUAL |
| HETEROSEXUALS | HOMOSEXUALS | EVERYONE REGARDLESS OF THEIR "BACKGROUND" | EVERYONE, SPECIAL BACKGROUNDS |
| BLUE COLLAR WORKERS | EMPLOYEES | MANAGERS | SELF-EMPLOYED |
| „SIMPLE" PEOPLE | "DIFFICULT" PEOPLE | BABIES | SMALL CHILDREN |
| SMALL GROUPS (<10) | LARGER GROUPS (>10) | POVERTY-STRICKEN | FEEBLE |
| WEALTHY | POWERFUL | OFFICIALS | MILITARY |
| HANDICAPPED | MENTALLY RETARDED | SICK PEOPLE IN GENERAL | ADDICTS |
| UNEDUCATED | NON ATHLETIC | OVERWEIGHT PERSONS | STRESSED OUT PEOPLE |
| RELIGIOUS | MISTREATED | RELATIONSHIP- DISTURBED | FINANCIALLY DISTURBED |
| FATHERS | MOTHERS | MARRIED COUPLES | SINGLES |

And again, the question to ask yourself: have I really circled all points honestly and spontaneously without letting my euphoria being influenced by fretting too long over the choices? Did I really follow my own personal beliefs keeping in mind it doesn't matter what I circle here because everything is equally well-paid or not at all and I don't need to worry if I get "a job" at all. I don't need to justify myself to anyone but myself. It's only about what would be the most fun if I chose it myself without having any kind of material dependency, envy, resentment, misunderstanding or other types of dependencies regarding existential questions. It's all here…I just need to grasp it to be happy. If I notice that I am already doing some of these things then that's even better for me. That means I am heading in the right direction.

This book is not meant to be your critic or your boss; it is a means to an end. It's the menu and the grill for a tasty barbeque plate consisting of qualities, needs, talents and abilities. We have to make ourselves constantly aware of these attributes. We are taking a field trip to our own inner self. Others bring a Guru home or go river rafting with their trainer on a homemade raft, singing motivating songs with their supervisor through the rapids just to prove themselves as indispensable or "Team oriented". But we are just reading a book, and we know there is only one person we can fool here… and I believe you know who we are talking about.

Now, enough of circling. We want to get down to details. Boil the chicken down to the broth to taste the essence of our own personally flavoured soup that will lead us down the right road.

# 09 | MY MAIN STRENGTHS AND ABILITIES

Ever heard of "focusing"? Exactly, we gather all our energy and clearly sharpen a certain point. Of course we all have some of the many before-mentioned qualities and needs in us and we also have a good feeling too about many of the concepts mentioned in each of the three skills charts. One feels drawn more to this one, the other more to that one, as explained before. The problem for most people though is that they have so many different abilities entwined that they don't know where or how to start.

Many perhaps just suspect what they do not want because we are influenced daily by the negative examples of life situations conveyed to us through mass media. What we can do the best, really want to do and how we can best reach this goal remains for most of us unclear. We only react but do not act. Good news: we are in the process of changing this!

Unfortunately, I don't know most of my readers personally, but one thing is for sure: whoever has openly and intensively occupied themselves with what they have read so far, has already become more creative and self-confident. If we're now sitting in front of a whole lot of circled words and thinking we're not smarter than before, well you're wrong. For you see, we have put together a clear package of all possibilities. We've become a whole lot clearer, have created a profile and retrieved our lost special qualities from our consciousness, back to our working memory so to speak, to have readily available for further processing.

If we are going to march in the most direct possible path to our personal "sunny side", then we should do that with the least amount of luggage to help preserve our energy. We will once again strike through our list mercilessly. We are now going to concentrate on nine of our strongest prominent qualities, needs and attributes from each of the six earlier charts. At the same time we are going to weigh out exactly which quality at the moment means the most to us personally. Which one do I want to concentrate on more? Which personal need is at this time greater to enable the optimal use of a valuable quality? Which of my personal abilities are the most pronounced and therefore would come closest to satisfying my needs for a longer period of time?

We take each of these nine with us, which doesn't mean that we still don't have the others. We just don't want to burden ourselves with them at this point because we want to take the shortest and most accurate path, like on a laser beam, in moving toward our goal. Got it? So, take all your charts and pick out nine of your strongest or most important qualities from each of the charts. We will only take these nine with us and jot them down in the appropriate slots on the following pages.

It is not a problem if someone has not circled more than nine points in any chart and for this there could be several reasons. Most likely here is someone who already has a clear picture of themselves with a targeted field of interest. These are for instance: people who are intensely interested in only a few themes and are therefore further advanced because they are already working to their full capacity. I will call them the "deep people". They are the opposites of "shallow people", who have more fields of interest but don't know their way through them as intensively or detailed. Both types are equally worthy, just simply different. Similar to tall slim trees often having long deep roots whereas broad trees tend to spread their roots widely along the surface to gain their foothold.

If we have only circled nine to ten items, or even less on most of the charts, then you should ask yourself if you were really being brave. Did you really circle everything that is, at least, of some interest to you?

It is possible, for whatever reason, that we are too "closed" and not daring enough to see what we really are capable of. Too closed to see what all could be possible in a fulfilling life because we possibly have never had the experience. In these cases it is helpful to ask what life circumstances in our past could have possibly influenced us not to allow these feelings or situations. It will then be clear that alone the fact that these possibilities were not available in the past is no reason why they cannot be a part of our future since you now have a say in the matter.

We wouldn't otherwise be in this situation – in which we have been thinking creatively about our past and our future – if we had not had the opportunity to find this book. Something must have previously changed in our thinking, which motivated us. At least for our own sake, we should learn to put these negative experiences aside. Strive on learning how to love yourself more, respect yourself and grant yourself a treat. Even if you have only little or no knowledge how to do this. Gratification and joy needs experience, time and routine. Your direction of thinking is the key!

Once again, remember that we are striking through all the earlier six charts of concepts/terms to sift out nine of our strongest or most important points from each chart. We will only refer to these right now and jot them down on the following blanks.

## MY NINE MAIN EMOTIONAL QUALITIES

..................................................    ..................................................

..................................................    ..................................................

..................................................    ..................................................

..................................................    ..................................................

..................................................

## MY NINE MAIN RATIONAL QUALITIES

..................................................    ..................................................

..................................................    ..................................................

..................................................    ..................................................

..................................................    ..................................................

..................................................

## MY NINE MAIN INDIVIDUAL NEEDS

..................................................    ..................................................

..................................................    ..................................................

..................................................    ..................................................

..................................................    ..................................................

..................................................

## MY NINE MAINLY PREFERRED THINGS OR MATERIALS

...........................................................................  ...........................................................................

...........................................................................  ...........................................................................

...........................................................................  ...........................................................................

...........................................................................  ...........................................................................

...........................................................................

## MY NINE MAINLY PREFERRED TYPES OF INFORMATION

...........................................................................  ...........................................................................

...........................................................................  ...........................................................................

...........................................................................  ...........................................................................

...........................................................................  ...........................................................................

...........................................................................

## MY NINE MAINLY PREFERRED TYPES OF PEOPLE

...........................................................................  ...........................................................................

...........................................................................  ...........................................................................

...........................................................................  ...........................................................................

...........................................................................  ...........................................................................

...........................................................................

So we have now narrowed the choices down. Slowly your image is taking place showing the beginning contours of a (your) personality. Admittedly we do not know exactly what person is hidden underneath or what his or her best qualities are. We can only guess, even though the author has already tortured us enough! In spite of this, we still have to persevere.

Again, remember it's not about throwing out already established qualities. It is about concentrating on the basics of a direct route on our way to the well-deserved goal that's called having a clear picture of our self. We know why we do something and what we are doing today. We accept this and know why we are here today. But we also know where we – according to our latest level of knowledge – want to go, could or should go, if we want to have more fun and ease, and experience more luck in life in our own manner. If we simply want to do more of what is "our thing"!

You think you are already finished? Oh no, not quite yet! We are going to get rid of more bulk and reduce down to our three most dominant characteristics that we will carefully weigh (what is more important to me?) and insert in the following blanks. At the same time we will evaluate our selection (if we haven't already done so) because now we are looking for the most obvious features of our personalities:

#1) in the following chart is every main characteristic (my personal #1) from each of both quality areas respectively my main need!

#2) is my second strongest (my personal #2) and

#3) my third strongest (my personal #3) quality or need.

We are getting down to the essence of a unique person – YOU. This is practical self-discovery. Dear talent scouts, your evaluation please!

## THESE THREE ARE MY MOST DOMINANT EMOTIONAL CHARACTERISTICS (QUALITIES). I AM THE CLOSEST TO BEING ...

1 | MOST PROMINENT ...........................................................................................................................

2 | SECOND MOST PROMINENT ...........................................................................................................

3 | THIRD MOST PROMINENT ..............................................................................................................

Carry on likewise for the next sections, until "type of people"!


## THESE ARE MY THREE MOST RATIONAL CHARACTERISTICS (QUALITIES). I AM THE CLOSEST TO BEING ...

1 | MOST PROMINENT ...........................................................................................................................

2 | SECOND MOST PROMINENT ...........................................................................................................

3 | THIRD MOST PROMINENT ..............................................................................................................


## THESE ARE MY MOST DOMINANT NEEDS.
## WHAT I NEED THE MOST IS ...

1 | MOST PROMINENT ...........................................................................................................................

2 | SECOND MOST PROMINENT ...........................................................................................................

3 | THIRD MOST PROMINENT ..............................................................................................................

## THESE THREE PREFERRED THINGS OR MATERIALS ARE THE MOST DOMINANT. WHAT I PREFER THE BEST ...

1 | MOST PROMINENT .................................................................................................................................

2 | SECOND MOST PROMINENT ...............................................................................................................

3 | THIRD MOST PROMINENT .....................................................................................................................


## THESE THREE TYPES OF INFORMATION (MEDIA) ARE THE MOST DOMINANT. WHAT I PREFER THE BEST ...

1 | MOST PROMINENT .................................................................................................................................

2 | SECOND MOST PROMINENT ...............................................................................................................

3 | THIRD MOST PROMINENT .....................................................................................................................


## FROM MY PREFERRED TYPES OF PEOPLE THESE ARE THE MOST DOMINANT. THESE TYPE OF PEOPLE INTEREST ME THE MOST ...

1 | MOST PROMINENT .................................................................................................................................

2 | SECOND MOST PROMINENT ...............................................................................................................

3 | THIRD MOST PROMINENT .....................................................................................................................

Finished! It may have seemed very tedious for some but it was pertinent that we did this in several steps. Whoever prefers to, can intermittently reduce the items from nine to five on a separate piece of paper. Experience shows that the result is much more accurate if you eliminate in several steps. To pick out three from a selection of 40 elements at one time would lead to inaccuracy. It is too easy to lose sight of the overview and therefore a satisfactory result is not possible because too many elements have to be weighed out against each other. We want to know precisely and not too hastily. We need to take our time. We are in the middle of life and not just in some job mediation. That is what we want to get away from!

# 10 | INTERIM RESULTS: "EVERYTHING AT A GLANCE"

From almost 300 personality characteristics regarding the areas of human traits, needs, talents and skills we have managed to sculpt a clear profile of our 18 typical characteristics in several steps that personify our special individuality. We have concentrated on those features that are either very important to us at this time, of great interest, or those that were perhaps already a successful element of our life.

To construct an even clearer picture of our hard-earned results let us recapitulate on the following page. In addition, we will circle in bold print the field that interests us the most, in other words, where we would most preferably like to utilize the accumulated "power" of our best quality!

Whoever is not completely sure can look back and ask themselves these following questions:
| Where did I circle the most elements?
| Which area was especially easy for me to complete?
| Where could I develop the most ideas?

In doing this we obtain a clearer picture of our personal identity at this point in our life. If someone were to ask you today who you are, you could give clear answers now. Many people do not achieve this all of their life!

The previous phase has been consciously prepared by deliberating our thoughts and written notes. Thus, each time we deal with this material and the resulting elements, we are also imprinting them deeper into our consciousness and subconscious.

Concurrently we have had plenty of opportunity to contemplate our personal preferences and qualities apart from any commercial value.

In doing so we were able to choose freely without having a special "quality" goal predestined for us because here it is only about spontaneous enthusiasm and individual tendencies. This is the only way to free development! Our interval summary will follow; our "Wanted" poster.

## MY MORE EMOTIONAL QUALITIES: I AM ...

1 | MOST PROMINENT ...........................................................................

2 | SECOND MOST PROMINENT ...........................................................................

3 | THIRD MOST PROMINENT ...........................................................................

## MY MORE RATIONAL QUALITIES: AND I AM ...

1 | MOST PROMINENT ...........................................................................

2 | SECOND MOST PROMINENT ...........................................................................

3 | THIRD MOST PROMINENT ...........................................................................

## MY MAIN NEEDS: MOST IMPORTANT TO ME IS ...

1 | MOST PROMINENT ...........................................................................

2 | SECOND MOST PROMINENT ...........................................................................

3 | THIRD MOST PROMINENT ...........................................................................

## THINGS/MATERIAL: I PREFER TO OCCUPY MYSELF WITH ...

1 | MOST PROMINENT ...........................................................................

2 | SECOND MOST PROMINENT ...........................................................................

3 | THIRD MOST PROMINENT ...........................................................................

## INFORMATION: I PROCESS INFORMATION PREFERABLY AS ...

1 | MOST PROMINENT ...........................................................................

2 | SECOND MOST PROMINENT ...........................................................................

3 | THIRD MOST PROMINENT ...........................................................................

# PEOPLE

AND I PREFER TO WORK WITH (OR FOR) ...

.................................................................................................................................

.................................................................................................................................

.................................................................................................................................

THE FIELD ...
O THINGS / MATERIALS
O  INFORMATION
O PEOPLE
... INTERESTS ME THE MOST.

THIS IS WHERE I CONCENTRATE MY ENERGY!

DATE / SIGNATURE ...........................................................................................................

This completed interim result should best be clearly "dog-eared" in your book. Better yet, make a photocopy and keep it in a place you see frequently, for example on your night table, bathroom mirror, or refrigerator. Have it ready to jog our memory. Depending on your situation naturally not provocatively in clear view, yet discreetly – for YOU!

We have created a manifest here. A fundamental revelation based on our current perspective of life. I thoroughly recommend mentioning these qualities in your resume or current job applications. When it comes to conveying a picture of the person behind this "technical data" we can offer a lot more than just an imageless, chummy "fulfillment aid". The power of spoken words supports us here, in our training camp, before we demonstrate our freshly gained knowledge tenuously to the public. Manifestation is an important part of the complex process of self-discovery in which we find ourselves at this moment.

Our next step is to find the next mirror and to read out loud to ourselves our interim results : " I am ….. and I am … Most important to me is …. I prefer to occupy myself with …. I process information preferably as …. I prefer to work with (or for) …… and the field … is where I want to concentrate my energy!"

Does this slip off your tongue easily? Are you convincing, are you convinced? Can you support what you are saying? Are we what we say we are, or at least believe that this status is worth striving for if we alone could decide? Whoever's not sure should start again from the beginning until the results are correct. Everyone else can take the next step and be confident that positive thinking is contingent with positive conduct and that equals positive success! Mirror, mirror on the wall ….. CHECK YOURSELF OUT!!

# 11 | REFLECTION AND SELF-AFFIRMATION

This will be of no use to those who cannot believe in the methods and knowledge practiced here. The others though, who have in the meantime achieved an idea of where all this can lead, will carry on. With the interim results of your own "wanted poster" in your pocket, you can deliver proof of what you have discovered in yourself. This proof serves on one side to reassess our previous results and ideally to confirm our beliefs. On the other hand the manifestation and documentation serve simultaneously as affirmation and positive reinforcement of our actions to attain our targeted goals. In turn, it all works together as further self affirmation to attain our new feelings of self esteem. "Encourage yourself". Moreover, this is also an important factor to reaching your goal.

Next to the three ascertained dominant characteristics from the six fields of your personality, write down convincing sentences relevant to certain situations in your live that proves you really embody the strongest of your known qualities. You will do this for at least each of your strongest qualities or characteristics (#1) from all six categories. If you can find affirming sentences for your second and third strongest characteristics, then you can deal with them more securely.

It's not so much about composing a well-formed sentence but rather about the deeper logic of the sentence. The "testimonial" actually consists of a group or set of logical consequences. First and foremost are your confirmed characteristics, followed by individual qualities, your "testimonial" and a conclusion. Take an extra piece of paper and roughly formulate your thoughts at first, then shorten the text, and finally refine it with precision.

We want to make logical deductions of past situations until they present themselves as a true chain of evidence we can pull on. It doesn't have to be a major event to be used as a testimony. Frequently these situations are easier than we think because we often take many of them for granted. Perhaps our unique way of thinking and handling of situations is the difference here that clearly defines our special worth? Our "testimonial" doesn't need to be based on actual deeds. It can be the isolated case where we would have handled a situation differently than we actually did in reality. Our goodwill was there but perhaps we didn't have the nerve, the energy or the chance to alter the situation as we would have preferred to. It could also be the "almost case" or good intentions in a situation where if given the opportunity we would take the chance to alter it. But first of all, look for real examples!

Remember, again it is important to write from a positive point of view. Don't just document what didn't happen or didn't work out, just mention what was the reason for success or what could have been the reason for success in these situations. Doing this, always write in the "I" form, i.e., not "one....", but "I ...". Enter real names and dates (not just "X" or "Y"! Take your time finding examples. Typically, some people can't think of anything fitting when they actively mull over it. If necessary, take a break from your attempt to solve this. The solution sometimes occurs to one spontaneously in a completely different situation, when the pressure of having to find it is gone. But when you do find it, better write it down quickly before your lose your grasp of it. Here's an example:

EXAMPLE  |  MY MAIN QUALITY IS "HONESTY"

The logical TESTIMONIAL of my life could possibly read like this: My friend asked me enthusiastically about my opinion on his brand new expensive car that really meant a lot to him. I told him point blank that I was happy for him but that this model didn't suit my taste and that I would have bought it in a different color.

CONCLUSION: It was an uncomfortable message but I said what I really thought. I didn't play a role for my friend just so he could get a quick – and false – feeling of confirmation, one that was not my honest opinion. I was simply being an honest friend!

Everything clear? The next examples are not explained in detail but should only serve as a security rope, like the ones you find on a narrow mountain trail. The actual creative effort should come from ourselves. Now, your turn:

MY EMOTIONAL QUALITIES are made evident in the following examples of my life that define and confirm my findings:

QUALITY 1 ....................................................................................................................................

EXAMPLE ....................................................................................................................................


QUALITY 2 ....................................................................................................................................

EXAMPLE ....................................................................................................................................


QUALITY 3 ....................................................................................................................................

EXAMPLE ....................................................................................................................................

## SECOND EXAMPLE | MY MAIN QUALITY IS "SELF-RELIANCE"

The *TESTIMONIAL* could look like this: I started a new job at company X. I received only a short introduction of my job duties and then was left alone to do my work. Without hesitation I approached my colleagues and supervisors who I questioned long enough until I knew exactly what my duties were and understood how to deal with the relevant data of my position. I determined who my contact persons were and could then start working sensibly.

CONCLUSION: I didn't wait till the work was delegated to me (or not), instead I immediately took matters into my own hands. I know how to help myself and don't wait for external help, I am self-reliant and at the same independent and free, but not thoughtless. Now it's your turn ….

My **RATIONAL QUALITIES** are made evident in the following examples of my life that define and confirm my findings:

QUALITY 1 ...............................................................................................................

EXAMPLE ...............................................................................................................

QUALITY 2 ...............................................................................................................

EXAMPLE ...............................................................................................................

QUALITY 3 ...............................................................................................................

EXAMPLE ...............................................................................................................

THIRD EXAMPLE: MY MAIN NEED IS "CONFIDENCE"

TESTIMONIAL: I booked a vacation last year at a singles resort in X just to be independent of others and to have time for myself. My partner is against it, doesn't trust me, is trying to convince me not to go and would rather spend the time with me. I'm disappointed because my partner is considering his/her own interests more than mine; doesn't support me nor trust me.

CONCLUSION: I need the trust of my partner to feel comfortable. And now your turn:

My MAIN NEEDS are made evident in the following examples of my life that define and confirm my findings:

NEED 1 ........................................................................................................................

EXAMPLE ..................................................................................................................

NEED 2 ........................................................................................................................

EXAMPLE ..................................................................................................................

NEED 3 ........................................................................................................................

EXAMPLE ..................................................................................................................

Just to mention again, it doesn't have to be some outstanding event that influences our testimonial. It's possible, but most likely it's the less significant situations in life we can fall back on as shown in the examples. The deciding factor is that we come to a logical conclusion where we gain clarity with respect to the causes and effects. We don't just figure out what the symptoms are, we want to really find the root of the matter. "Why is it that I am gladly ....., especially in need of ....., or can do well? The closer we get to the root of what is good for us and "how we can do well", the better we can plan to reach our goal and the bigger our chance that we really will achieve it!

The situation is similar in the following three themes of What, How and Why we enjoy or would enjoy doing something. Based on a general indication we are feeling our way closer to the exact activity we really like or one we feel we could like even if we have had no experience in this field or have just toyed with the idea.

So if we don't have any experience with what we find intuitively worth striving for, then let us try to fantasize a bit more. Let's pretend to be in a desired situation. We are simply "dreaming" and see it taking place in our mind's eye. Because dreams are the core of our success!

Now then, "Functionaries into the country" (said Mao Tse Tung), go to your field of activity! We will now concentrate on what we can do, like to do, and what we would like to learn to do. Search your soul, as usual!

EXAMPLE: CLOTHING

TESTIMONIAL: children's clothing > exclusive children's clothing> designing exclusive children's clothing > design exclusive children's clothing in style X and quality Y.

CONCLUSION: I would like to design clothes for children in a particular style and quality so they will feel comfortable in them. I like children and my understanding of attractive clothing will meet the requirements of my target group. Now You:

MY MAIN INTERESTS IN THINGS OR MATERIALS are made evident in the following examples of my life that define and confirm my findings:

THINGS/MATERIALS 1 ...........................................................................................

EXAMPLE ...........................................................................................................

THINGS/MATERIALS 2 ...........................................................................................

EXAMPLE ...........................................................................................................

THINGS/MATERIALS 3 ...........................................................................................

EXAMPLE ...........................................................................................................

EXAMPLE: "CONSULTANCY"

TESTIMONIAL: Property Appraisal > residential property appraisal > analyze residential property appraisals to obtain their true value and help others get good value for their money.

CONCLUSION: I want to work independently and customer oriented to provide people with more price consciousness and satisfaction in the real estate business thereby obtaining a clear conscious while earning a living that creates better quality of life.

MY MAIN INTEREST IN PROCESSING OF INFORMATION (giving or taking) is made evident in the following examples of my life that define and confirm my findings:

TYPE OF INFORMATION 1 ...........................................................................................

EXAMPLE ...........................................................................................................................

TYPE OF INFORMATION 2 ...........................................................................................

EXAMPLE ...........    ...........................................................................................................

TYPE OF INFORMATION 3 ...........................................................................................

EXAMPLE ...........................................................................................................................

EXAMPLE: "LOWER INCOME"

TESTIMONIAL: Lower income > lower income mothers > help lower-income single mothers balance full-time child care and leisure time.

CONCLUSION: I know that single mothers often find themselves in a dilemma without a concept for a satisfying compromise. I want to promote better conditions for happier mothers and happier children thus creating a better quality of life in general.

MY MAIN INTEREST IN WORKING WITH PEOPLE has made itself evident in the following examples of my life that define and confirm my findings:

TYPES OF PEOPLE 1 ....................................................................................................

EXAMPLE ................................................................................................................................

TYPES OF PEOPLE 2 ....................................................................................................

EXAMPLE ................................................................................................................................

TYPES OF PEOPLE 3 ....................................................................................................

EXAMPLE ................................................................................................................................

Got it? Check one more time: did I actively write in a positive sense instead of negatively (i.e., have not, did not want, did not). Did I correctly assess situations?

If we have found a logical (to us) Testimonial for at least every main quality (#1) then we have taken an additional critical step in the direction of self-confidence and clarity. That should be the least of what we accomplish. We have concrete documentation on what a difference our best characteristics make! Furthermore, whoever has managed to write down a testimonial for his second and third strongest qualities (#2 and #3), is even more secure in his new "old skin".

And even if some ask themselves "what's the point?", we should always remind ourselves what this book is about: to follow your calling! A status that goes way beyond the common human masses of those administrative idiots or other stoic and dependent "employees" who stumble in daily to a soulless office building.

Like researchers involved in a scientific project, we want to discover exactly where our path in life is going so that the remaining time of our earthly existence with all its ups and downs can be fully appreciated. To no longer "piddle" aimlessly through your media-controlled life being thankful for every handout of a merciful boss, humiliating yourself into yet another dependency.

Everything that we are discovering about ourselves makes us stronger – equal to other real businessman in "business life" – and gives us more self-esteem. Only if you believe in yourself will you be able to work well and with contentment.

# 12 | MY FIRST STEP TOWARDS FULFILLMENT

We still have one difficult task ahead of us. I would venture to say it's the most difficult in this book aside from basic will and capability. It's the first step to success; being completely honest with yourself.

This chapter is rich in content but because we are moving along so well, have learned so much about ourselves and are slowly reaching the core of our being, we have one more task. The task of creating a pretty colorful patchwork quilt with our own individual pattern made from those scraps of material, which contain our qualities, needs, talents and skills. This involves some effort, but when finished, it will have been well worth the trouble. We will have attained the basis for our long-term satisfying life recipe with the needed ingredients, which allow our best qualities to work towards our general well being.

This doesn't mean that everything else will come automatically, but the basic direction of your goal will be clear. Let's slip on our new "quality shoes" and take our first real steps. In doing so we must follow some rules so we don't slip and break our neck or possibly break our shoes in wrong. Make your notes based on the following method:

/ clear and active: I do (not: "one" does)
/ in the present: NOW! (not: „sometime")
/ use only POSITIVE terms (not: don't want to … )
/ use active words: accomplish….develop….enjoy….design…. compile….create….establish… assemble.....prepare
/ leave the beginning and end of our "story" open
/ avoid limitations by mentioning company or brand names, time constrictions, date of the year, location, etc.
/ for every theme, write down the first step

/ if we can think of more than one step then that's even better!
/ firstly we will address "what interests me the most" from the
  field Things/Materials, Information or People
/ it's great if we can find the first step to the other two fields –
  (to keep them in reserve) but it's not absolutely necessary.
/ we consolidate our "story" as much as possible in a second step
  without losing the basic idea so that the contents become clearer.
  "Simplify" is the answer (Simplify!....Your Life"), not only because you
  will find the root in a brief statement, but often the clarity.
/ WE ARE COMPLETING THIS TASK ENTIRELY UNTIL WE REACH AN ALL
  AROUND SATISFACTORY CONCLUSION – BECAUSE THIS IS OUR AREA
  OF ACTION FOR OUR FUTURE SUCCESS AND OUR LONG-TERM S
  ATISFACTION IN LIFE!!

Because we now know which of the three fields "Things/Materials,
Information or People" is right for us, we better take our conclusion
from page 69 as well as a separate piece of paper (or type it up separately on the computer) to answer two further questions regarding
what we have already discovered about ourselves. Whoever finds
a clear line of occupation or a definite job description, good. But
it's not a prerequisite, for this is about describing a field of activity in
which we can Image our talents and skills being adequately realized.

That doesn't mean it has to be an already established type of occupation! We can "create" our occupation! Just think about types of
occupations that are relatively young and were established in the last
twenty years. To name a few: "Environmental protectors", "Webmas-
ter" or "Change Manager". I'm talking about occupations that have
been derived from personal conviction towards social or technical
developments.

People have thoughts, feelings and ideas about certain situations or themes they have focused on and developed into imaginary fields of activity in which they can actively realize their concepts as well as make the most of their talents. This is how changes come into being and development takes place!

Perhaps we already have solutions to life and we're just waiting for someone to give us the chance to realize them! To be in the "right place at the right time", so to speak. Perhaps till now, the ratio of chance to risk allowing us to become the missile of world history, was just out of proportion. If you have the self-confidence, the chance is always there, no matter what the circumstances are!

Our next question is: Within a field that interests me most, in what position can I apply my main qualities, talents and skills and which needs should be ideally fulfilled to enable me to work successfully? From my own personal perspective, where would I fit in ideally and have the most fun? What do I trust myself to do the best? This is what we are looking for!! And we are thinking about what role we would like to conquer when we have enough experience, influence or whatever makes you mature enough for you to achieve this position.

Let's take the example of the former German Chancellor, Gerhard Schröder in 2004. It's been said that long before he attained this position he had been banging on the door of the chancellery at night demanding to be let in. His goal was clear! Years later when he made it he must have surely thought he was the ideal person for the job – a significant aspect of his self-confidence! The rest is history.

So another question you need to ask yourselves is this: What goal would I gladly want to work up to? With that applies: think positive!! "Think BIG !!

The core questions we want to find answers to are:

1 | I now recognize my main qualities and needs as well as what field interests me the most. With this knowledge, what state of affairs must I strive for – in my opinion – to be successful and happy in the long run and thus fulfill my purpose in life?

2 | From my current perspective, what could be my first definite step in the direction of reaching this fundamentally described state?

For this reason we are now going to address our individual qualities, needs, talents and skills and fuse these individual results into a Testimonial (in the form of a short paragraph or story).

Next, we will only answer partially otherwise it easily becomes too complex so better go step by step. First of all describe, in general, a condition or permanent life situation you would like to attain and then name specifically the first step you must take in the direction of reaching your own personal goal. Let's go:

01 | To use my MAIN QUALITIES intensively for my own individual happiness and satisfaction I must do the following:

....................................................................................................

....................................................................................................

....................................................................................................

Description (each one on an extra piece of paper!):

....................................................................................................

....................................................................................................

....................................................................................................

My first step towards this is:

....................................................................................................

....................................................................................................

....................................................................................................

02 | And to fulfill my MAIN NEEDS I must do the following:

....................................................................................................

....................................................................................................

....................................................................................................

Description:

....................................................................................................

....................................................................................................

....................................................................................................

My first step towards this is (select 3a, 3b or 3c):

..................................................................................................................

..................................................................................................................

..................................................................................................................

03a | To work with THINGS OR MATERIALS that I prefer the best,
      I must do the following:

..................................................................................................................

..................................................................................................................

..................................................................................................................

Description:

..................................................................................................................

..................................................................................................................

..................................................................................................................

My first step towards this is:

..................................................................................................................

..................................................................................................................

..................................................................................................................

03B | To work with INFORMATION that I prefer the best, I must
      do the following:

..................................................................................................................

..................................................................................................................

..................................................................................................................

Description:

.................................................................................................................

.................................................................................................................

.................................................................................................................

My first step towards this is:

.................................................................................................................

.................................................................................................................

.................................................................................................................

03C | To work with PEOPLE, the way I like it most, I must
do the following:

.................................................................................................................

.................................................................................................................

.................................................................................................................

Description:

.................................................................................................................

.................................................................................................................

.................................................................................................................

My first step towards this is:

.................................................................................................................

.................................................................................................................

.................................................................................................................

I don't give you an example for each individual step because you're very well capable of finding creative solutions and describing situations that need fulfillment to clarify your own individual qualities and needs. But I will give you an example of what kind of answer this should lead to, because in the second step you should be able to combine all your individual answers into one decisive statement that either consists of all the individual points or takes them into consideration. For example, in 1994 I was the managing director of an exclusive company in the home furnishing industry. Due to my inner dissatisfaction (I felt something was missing), and within the scope of my developing self-discovery I was able to patch together my "testimonial" based on the knowledge of my individual patchwork pieces and shortened it appropriately:

"I will create an independent, creative, responsible and outgoing job that is at the same time educational, official, caring, guiding and humane. One where, from a combination of learning, speaking and writing, I can make enough money to live on comfortably, and a little more."

With this "testimonial" tailored from all these single pieces of material I had, for the first time in my life, actively and precisely formulated what my occupational field must be to find long term happiness without limiting myself. I now had a clear picture in front of me and knew what I was looking for! Of course, this testimonial was the essence of somewhat much longer, when I started to formulate it and it took me quite some time (a few hours of thinking it over and shaping it) to write the above statement down.

For your information: I had worked in management jobs in sales for over ten years in various business firms, merchandising or production companies! I decided: In the future, I would orient my career

ambitions based on whether the appropriate position would encom-
pass all or most of the elements of my insight.

Now I only needed to take the first step. I set about it quite naively
and told myself that when studying the vacancies not to look at job
positions I would have normally applied for. Instead, I started looking
at jobs that would fit my relevant ideals, regardless of where. If I did
look at the old positions then only to consider them in a new aspect
as described above. This is how I finally took the first step to a new
sphere of self-consciousness beyond my existing world of thinking in
sales categories. Here's what I wrote:

"My first step: I will concentrate my energy on jobs in the field of
learning, teaching and writing and will try to acquire more practice
in these fields. At the same time I will inform myself on what type of
jobs are available in these fields and then apply for all the applicable
job openings in these fields that make sense and where I could gain
experience."

That was it! I simply looked at the world from a different standpoint;
ten inches away from my existing point of view regarding my life till
then…."my father was a businessman, my grandfather was a businessman…." Just say "yes" instead of "yes, but…." I was truly relieved
and had the feeling that a heavy burden had been taken off my
shoulders, one I was not aware of before. This is how I became the
distribution manager of a publishing company (reading and writing)
in 1996. I then worked for a company that rented vacation homes in
Denmark (people and contact) and after that as an editor for a well-
known Encyclopedia (speaking and writing). In 1999 I landed my first
job as a teacher in an institute for teaching adolescents.

After that, I worked first as an assistant, then later as a "permanent freelancer" and application training project manager in a large German training institute (official, guiding, educational and humane).

In my first teaching position I had answered an ad for a "business administration student to teach as a temporary..." I really didn't fit the job description except for the fact that I was interested in the further education of teenagers and young adults. I had actually dismissed the idea of having a chance at the job when I received a phone call in the car from the director of the youth education department asking me to come in for an interview. The pivotal point in me getting the job was my vast experience in various types of businesses and fields of occupation. I was therefore naturally at least one step ahead of my "normal" colleagues.

So, suddenly I was an official lecturer and teacher. This was a wish I actually already had when I was fourteen, but had dismissed due to the image I knew of teachers and their daily routine. It didn't hold a special attraction for me in the long run. The idea of having my lunch from a plastic lunchbox with other teachers in the teacher's lounge five days a week, year after year, did not appeal to me. I was looking for another style of teaching, but had no plan what it could be because as a fourteen year old I was too much in love with my life to give my calling any thought. My calling back then was closer to being the "clown of the class", whereby from my standpoint today I could see my intention was to make others happy.

In view of my new knowledge I then applied myself actively and consciously in my fields of interest and still continue to do so by constantly gaining new insights through different jobs, new and clearer perspectives of my special calling, my personal "purpose of life". In 1999

I rethought and rewrote my formerly defined skills and since then have been happily working from my "home-office". My writing and speaking skills, in particular, have crystallized distinctively and I recognized my need to be internationally active in order to achieve my long-term happiness. I am increasingly fascinated with human beings, personalities and the environment. I am evolving into a competent expert in this field by taking part in all imaginable functions and "stuffing" myself with any knowledge I can get my hands on regarding this theme. At the same time I feel with more clarity the joy I receive from learning and observe what an array of knowledge we have free at our disposal – if we just take advantage of it. Magnificent!

I am encouraging you again to first of all highlight the acquired individual components and then somehow bind them together to form your "testimonial", even if it is a bit clumsy at first. Then comes the fine-tuning and – most importantly – force yourself, to write down that first step that will take you in the direction of fulfillment, at least for the conclusion! If you should have a block while you are shortening or ironing out your text, leave it alone for a couple of hours or even a day. Take a walk! This could open your eyes.

Completion is the device here that will help you find the basis! All other thoughts and actions will develop automatically within the framework of your new knowledge. Whoever feels they are still missing reasons and substance after this exercise, well, they could be right. In the following two chapters you will be given many more possibilities to clarify your own personal viewpoint and direction.

# 13 | MY IDEA OF ACCOMPLISHMENT AND RISK

In this chapter, we will only address our self-esteem. Alone in a peaceful atmosphere delve into a deep state of self-awareness and with an optimistic attitude. We are in the "preserve" of this self-discovery book, named "Follow your Calling" and we will now have the opportunity to expand our opinion and viewpoint on two decisive questions that will significantly influence our actions: motivation and the willingness to take risks!

Our answers to these questions form a defined profile of our persona-lity that allow us to make clear decisions and take assertive action in our search for personal happiness in life. We are seeking great ideas, dreams or anything else, as long as we are honest with ourselves therefore making them essentially attainable. Doubt derived from failures of the past or fear of success in the future will not get us any further. Let your judgment be spontaneous and from the heart. There is no one who has never made a mistake or believed he had a special problem that only affected him. Until they looked around and found that no one is ever alone with their problems and that all problems have similar causes that can be solved.

It is important that the steps to accomplishment and risks in the next chapter are made based on your general life philosophy as well as your self-confidence and self-respect.

/ regardless of how often we have "fell flat on our face",
/ regardless of how often others have told us how dumb we are
/ regardless of what others think of us, in general, as a person
/ regardless how popular or unpopular your attitude is
    towards whatever

Whoever has a tendency to become depressed or has an especially hard time answering questions regarding life philosophy, thinking profoundly or positively, should put on some cheerful music before and pay close attention to the lyrics.

My recommendation would be something like "I AM WHAT I AM!" from GLORIA GAYNOR, "MY WAY" from FRANK SINATRA or "THIS IS MY LIFE" from SHIRLEY BASSEY. These titles work wonders for me spontaneously, brighten up the soul and allow me to think big – no matter what the weather is like outside! But I know there are always those recurring songs for every generation that give us encouragement, perhaps today more than ever! Pick out the songs or artists that give you courage and from whom you can say: "Yes, they believed in themselves, stayed true to themselves and found their way – even though the road was not always smooth. Whatever he or she is singing, I can relate to, and the same can apply to me!

So, think hard (smart) and prove to yourself that you actually already have the answers to your life's questions. We don't always have to look for confirmation from others or justify ourselves in what we do or want to do (or not). We just have to be true to ourselves and base our actions on basic valid principles!

Write your answers down please, at least in key words! In all respects, the core of the question we want to find an answer to is always "Why?". Take your time, and delve. We will go through the checklist:

/ What is my understanding of the phrase "good accomplishment"?

/ What kind of satisfaction do I expect from my own good accomplishment?

/ For what reason am I annoyed when I do not accomplish something?

/ How do I react when I do not accomplish what others expect from me?

/ How do I react when others do not accomplish what I expect from them?

/ What do my parents expect me to accomplish?

/ What do I expect my children to accomplish?

/ What was the most significant accomplishment in my life?

/ What type of accomplishment do I want to be remembered for when I die?

/ Is it fundamentally important to me, to be remembered for my accomplishments after death?

We have answered these questions based on what we think an accomplishment is, under what circumstances we are prepared to accomplish this, and what type of accomplishment is relevant to us. We have just defined a part of our world values and now the path is free for us to perform within our framework of accomplishment.

Our motives are now apparent. If we were honest with ourselves, then the subsequent action to be taken should be apparent too.

Now we have to ask ourselves what risks we are willing to take in our determination for performance.

/ What is my understanding of "taking a risk"?

/ Under what circumstances would I take a risk?

/ What appeals to me about taking a risk?

/ How do I react when others expect me to take a risk I am not ready for?

/ How do I react when others are not willing to take a risk I expect of them?

/ What type of risks do my parents expect me to take?

/ What type of risks do I expect my children to take?

/ In what situation did I take my biggest risk?

/ After my death, would I want to be remembered for my willingness to take risks?

/ Is it fundamentally important to me being remembered as one that was willing to take risks?


True enough, answering these twenty similar questions could scare some of us off but we are dealing with essential positions in our lives and personalities. If we can find the answers to these questions we can create more pleasure in our lives because again we have simply become clearer in our minds and therefore more definite and trans- lucent in our future decisions and conduct. We haven't committed ourselves one-sidedly with our answers to perception of personal accomplishments and risks. Instead we have brought more insight to our self-awareness to enable us to work goal-oriented. We have now set energy free for the implementation of our beliefs and purpose of life. This makes us likewise independent and resistant to outer influences. Further energy is saved by not wasting time on doubts; instead we have more time for serenity, personal activities and the joy of living.

But we can't be completely satisfied with ourselves just yet. Now that we've started we willcontinue with more essential questions that illuminate our personality from a few more critical perspectives. We will ask ourselves all those pertinent questions we have been carrying around in our sub-consciousness. Questions we will have to deal with one day anyway, but are asking ourselves now. We will then have an answer prepared and can deal with this special situation more confidently.

Moreover, answering some of the following questions will impart a self-confidence that will reveal the direction of our future dealings. The more we address our newly found knowledge, the more confident and lucid we become, inside and out.

Remember: with this knowledge, we have a considerable advantage over the great mass of humanity. It is the ability not only to just say "no" to what you find undesirable but the ability to consciously create the present and future.

Our belief in something is fundamental to reaching our goal. Whatever the mind can think of, it can achieve! Countless inventions and progress are the best examples of this.

# 14 | MY PHILOSOPHY OF LIFE IN KEY WORDS

We are now going to dedicate ourselves to answering essential questions about our ideas on reality and what we expect from life. Read the questions closely, think about it briefly and then write your spontaneous answers down in key words. You may not be sure you understood some of the questions correctly, so just write down the first answer that comes to your mind. That is the right answer!

REALITY        What is the difference between reality and truth?

CAUSES         Why do events/incidents happen the way they happen?

CHOICES        How do I reach decisions and what effects do they have?

ROLE MODEL  How would I like to be? Who are my idols?

PRINCIPLES   What are my fundamental beliefs? What do I stand for?

EGO            What do I think and what do I expect of myself?

SECURITY       How much security can I count on in my life?

SUCCESS        What is my definition of success?

SACRIFICE      What is a sacrifice?
               What would I be willing to sacrifice something for?

VALUES         What makes my life precious in the long run?

| | |
|---|---|
| HAPPINESS | What does "happiness" mean to me? |
| RESPONSIBILITY | Who is responsible for my life happiness? |
| BELIEFS | What do I truly believe in? |
| HOPE | What does hope mean to me? |
| LOVE | What is love?<br>What does it mean to me?<br>How do I show love? |
| HIGHEST ENTITY | Do I believe in any kind of God?<br>What is my "God" like? |
| EARTH | What is the biggest problem on our earth<br>(in the world)? |
| HUMANITY | What is actually the one special quality of humanity? |
| BEHAVIOR | How must we (all of us) behave for a peaceful<br>coexistence? |
| COMMUNITY | How must we deal with each other so community<br>can be fulfillment? |
| GOALS | What could be a collective goal for all humans? |
| BENEFIT | How could I help to achieve this collective goal? |
| CONTENT | Ideally, what should I do with my talent? |
| DEATH | What are my feelings on death? |
| MEANING | The purpose of my life is … |

What was that? More questions, even more insight! I know, your "brain is smoking", but again we have playfully managed to drive several stakes into the ground for a solid foundation. For every person that exists, there are just as many right solutions, but they have to basically correspond with each other. Otherwise the world wouldn't function permanently.

The sooner people develop this insight and communicate it the sooner they can improve the situation for themselves and others in the world. Up until this point you have:

/ Established and written down your feelings about individual accomplishment and risk to develop your own real work philosophy.

/ Manifested and called into consciousness your own individual basic values for a long lasting, steady life philosophy in a world of ever and faster changing "truths".

/ Simultaneously defined general basic values that are valid for harmonious cooperation (think about the German philosopher Kant's "categorical imperative")

/ Gone from being insecure and disoriented to having developed security and strength through defining values and goals

/ Identified, analyzed and if necessary, eliminated your own mental blocks and strategies of avoidance

/ Created a solution-oriented testimonial:
What good can I do, what should I do and what will I do?

This is another important step away from widely propagandized, media-controlled and materialistic values of those producers who profit from their message "Consumption = Happiness!" to the aimless, fumbling mass of passive followers strapped in their corset of dependencies.

The point of this concentrated sequence of exercises and self-analysis is to develop your own way of thinking and your own profile; to become a "trendsetter" instead of a "trend follower" and submissive consumer.

It's exactly like getting your driver's license. Only in daily traffic do we gain routine and experience.

Some people have gained insight only after several sessions with their expensive psychologist or other counselor, who has, in the end, only served as a catalyst to free us from our own prison and related mental blocks.

We have defined our qualities, our needs, our talents and our skills. These have contributed to a clear profile with a goal-oriented field of occupation. We have then consciously reassessed the whole thing again and personally searched for our own holistic philosophy:

If we could achieve everything we have discovered about ourselves (and most likely achieve very well), when the conditions are right, then what could we imagine to achieve or accomplish above and beyond this? What is our criterion for this and in what direction should the world evolve so that we, and future generations, can speak of progress as defined by mankind? All these questions have now been partially clarified, yet time will give us more opportunity to deliberate, to handle appropriately, to experiment and become even more secure.

In the following chapter we will take our newly found fundamental knowledge and turn it into our own personal, tangible life goal. At the same time we will construct a life plan that can be ideally executed. Some may find this to be exaggerated or "artificial". But whoever has no goal, will never be able to consciously reach that goal.

And if one does not calculate at least a general time frame for these goals to be reached, this person will eventually be plagued with vague concepts and diffused prospects, which will probably never be realized. They will drag themselves through the reality of each day without prospect. These are exactly the visionless fantasists that we all know. People who are often negative because they have no strategic concept. Sad figures!

Nevertheless, it doesn't mean we must adhere meticulously to our once established plan without regard for losses, no matter what happens. That could be, in some cases, fatal. What's important is to have a framework of action ready at a particular point in time that we can immediately navigate in the direction of our goal. We will adapt our plan to fit our realistic needs in the course of time, depending on what happens. We don't want to create a complicated plan that investigates all feasible eventualities, which could possibly limit our creativity and hinder our actions. For instance, that would be exactly why, in my opinion, so little changes in the world.

This is primarily about a framework of action with a time requirement for ourselves, a personal guideline, so to speak. We are becoming ultra quick effective planers now. CONGRATULATIONS!

# 15 | MY GOAL IN LIFE AND MY LIFE SCHEME

## "IT IS NOT ENOUGH TO KNOW, YOU MUST USE THAT KNOWLEDGE. IT IS NOT ENOUGH TO WANT, YOU MUST ALSO ACT."

Goethe

Actually I had consciously abstained from using quotes but Goethe (again) fits here perfectly. Somehow it has all been said before and it's the duty of people like me to modernize it and newly communicate that ancient wisdom. One more time to make sure it sinks in: To reach my goals, I must know my goals, although I know my goals could change at any time. I don't have to commit myself for a lifetime right now. Whoever has no goal, cannot consciously meet one and can easily become the instrument of others for their goals. The best example for this is your typical media oriented consumer that lets himself be led by the latest, most intensively advertised "trends" and still wonders (if at all) why everyone else is earning off him but himself.

That's why we will actively define, based on the following eight sectors of our lives, our very personal goals that can be achieved in a feasible time period. This is about imagining and writing down what state of affairs we want to have reached at a certain point of time. Therefore, again we will write actively and positively in the present tense. Imagine yourselves in the respective situation – now!

Next of all I would like to explain the terms regarding the eight life sectors in greater detail.

WORK

What do we have accomplished in our working life, in our profession, or with regard to our personal "calling"?

LEISURE

How do we spend our leisure time? Which hobbies or other interests do we pursue?

RELATIONSHIP

What type of relationship do we have with our life partner (the person we will experience life with)? Not only formally, but with respect to the contents?

FAMILY / FRIENDS

What kind of relationship do we have with our parents, siblings, children, other relatives and friends?

HOME

What is our home like? For instance, the area we live in. What does it look like and how do we style our home?

BODY

In what kind of condition do we keep our body? What do we expect of ourselves physically?

SPIRIT

What kind of awareness and spiritual quality have we developed? What and how do we learn?

SOUL

What level of spiritual awareness (beyond the known facts) have we reached? Have we entered into an individual relationship with faith? How will this take form and in what do we believe?

We will be answering exactly these questions in the next six charts. In the first chart we will review what we have accomplished in these areas up until this point. What stage have we developed to in these named points, so far? What is the "status quo"?

Like a well-meaning good friend, we will now try to take a position in which we can observe our current life from a clear viewpoint and make notes on our "I am"-state in these eight life sectors. We will enter the results, preferably in creative sentences, in Chart 1).

Then Chart 2) and 3) follow in the same manner and in the exact order given. This is important! Just to look back once: "What was our past like"? "What is now"? And "what shall our future look like"? Then we will already have a comparison with our past, present and future!

Please insert in all the charts here your corresponding age and the exact date of the designated point in time so you can name this time exactly as a target to later review your success: "what has happened"?

The charts 4) to 6) are to be, of course, filled out with exact data and according to the applicable scheme but based on this premise: "What do I have to do or what do I have to have accomplished by the designated date and age here so I can reach the desired state at the appropriate time?" as mentioned in table 3), i.e. in 12 years!

Please take sufficient time and have plenty of room for these charts but fill them out, if possible, in one go so you stay concentrated and immersed in the theme. Describe the essentials of the eight sectors from which you want your life happiness to be measured by.

FOLLOW YOUR INTUITION!

1 | INVENTORY | AT THIS TIME (today, NOW)
I am in the following situation regarding these eight sectors of my life:

WORK

.....................................................................................................................................

LEISURE

.....................................................................................................................................

RELATIONSHIP

.....................................................................................................................................

FAMILY/FRIENDS

.....................................................................................................................................

HOME

.....................................................................................................................................

BODY

.....................................................................................................................................

SPIRIT

.....................................................................................................................................

SOUL

.....................................................................................................................................


MY AGE TODAY IS      ................................................................................................
THE EXACT DATE NOW ................................................................................................

## 2 | LOOKING BACK: 12 MONTHS AGO

I was in the following situation regarding these eight sectors of my life:

WORK

..............................................    ...................................................................................................................

LEISURE

...................................................................................................................................................................................

RELATIONSHIP

...................................................................................................................................................................................

FAMILY/FRIENDS

...................................................................................................................................................................................

HOME

...................................................................................................................................................................................

BODY

...................................................................................................................................................................................

SPIRIT

...................................................................................................................................................................................

SOUL

...................................................................................................................................................................................

MY AGE 12 MONTH AGO    .........................................................................................................

THE EXACT DATE THEN    .........................................................................................................

## 3 | LONG-TERM PLAN: IN 12 YEARS
I will be in the following situation regarding these eight sectors of my life:

WORK

..................................................................................................................................

LEISURE

..................................................................................................................................

RELATIONSHIP

..................................................................................................................................

FAMILY/FRIENDS

..................................................................................................................................

HOME

..................................................................................................................................

BODY

..................................................................................................................................

SPIRIT

..................................................................................................................................

SOUL

..................................................................................................................................

MY AGE IN 12 YEARS ......................................................................................................

THE EXACT DATE THEN ..................................................................................................

## 4 | MID-TERM PLAN: IN 12 MONTHS

To reach my 12-months-plan I will be in the following situation regarding these eight sectors of my life:

WORK

.................................................................................................................

LEISURE

.................................................................................................................

RELATIONSHIP

.................................................................................................................

FAMILY/FRIENDS

.................................................................................................................

HOME

.................................................................................................................

BODY

.................................................................................................................

SPIRIT

.................................................................................................................

SOUL

.................................................................................................................

MY AGE IN 12 MONTH ....................................................................................

THE EXACT DATE THEN ....................................................................................

## 5 | SHORT-TERM PLAN IN 12 WEEKS
To reach my 12-months-plan I will be in the following situation regarding these eight sectors of my life:

WORK

..................................................................................................................................

LEISURE

..................................................................................................................................

RELATIONSHIP

..................................................................................................................................

FAMILY/FRIENDS

..................................................................................................................................

HOME

..................................................................................................................................

BODY

..................................................................................................................................

SPIRIT

..................................................................................................................................

SOUL

..................................................................................................................................


MY AGE IN 12 WEEKS .............................................................................................

THE EXACT DATE THEN .........................................................................................

## 6 | IMMEDIATE PLAN: IN 12 DAYS

To reach my 12-weeks-plan I will be in the following situation regarding these eight sectors of my life:

WORK

......................................................................................................................

LEISURE

......................................................................................................................

RELATIONSHIP

......................................................................................................................

FAMILY/FRIENDS

......................................................................................................................

HOME

......................................................................................................................

BODY

.....................................................    .................................................

SPIRIT

......................................................................................................................

SOUL

......................................................................................................................


MY AGE IN 12 DAYS      ...........................................................................

THE EXACT DATE THEN    ...........................................................................

So let's first take inventory for our successful life planning, for the present day. Deadline: today!

Then we look back on how our situation has changed within the last twelve months to get a better feel of the changes possible in the time span of a year. Ultimately however, we want to think about the future and get a clue of what was – for example – possible within a year!

Perhaps we already have our own effective life plan in operation and have just fine-tuned it? Even then it's good to have this clear in our head, so at this point we could probably name further goals that we want to reach. But perhaps our situation has become worse through aimlessness and lack of motivation? Then it is high time to think about how we change this situation!

In the third part of the plan we have written down what we want to have accomplished in 12 years. This demands a considerable amount of concentration and imagination, but it is very important that we abandon ourselves to this vision. To even roughly reach this, we will probably have to take appropriate action at short notice, (for example within twelve days) to set the course that will lead us to our goals on schedule. Those who are completely determined will take action within twelve hours!

If we do this, we should have results within twelve weeks, i.e., three months later. We will enter these results into our corresponding chart and if after twelve weeks our situation has evolved as a result of our actions, then we will  experience even further development in four times that period i.e., a year! The plan had to be worked backwards though because experience has shown it is easier to visualize and plan starting with the most distant steps in the future. This, in turn, enables short-term planning of the necessary interim stations to fall into place.

Basically, it's about calculating what we can and want to demand of ourselves within these timeframes, i.e., what we believe we must do by a certain point in time to reach our ultimate goal. The exact dates and our corresponding age at that time will help boost our imagination. This is the red thread, which we can follow. Thus we are making our life plan our business; the business of being our own boss!

What we do and how far we implement our plan afterwards, as well as how good we manage and lead our own life depends, largely, on us. It depends on our self-discipline, the quality of our decisions, our steadfastness and of course, the experience we have gained on the way. For many of us this carefully researched chart will probably be the first time we have ever held an extensive plan like this in our hands; one that can guide us in the right direction and reveal what course of action to take.

Many speak of "retirement" or "twilight years", but most people do not have the slightest idea of how they should specifically structure this time of their life or how much effort it will take to really experience it, as they would like to experience it. Even so, the time up until retirement doesn't necessarily have to be a torturous or humiliating experience. Not at all!

Of course, luck always plays a major role, but I tend to more and more believe that luck is bestowed upon the positive thinker ...

# 16 | MY NEW BUSINESS CARD: "WHO I REALLY AM"

Now that we have done thorough life planning, it's time to make a new calling card for ourselves, a "Testimony" that will describe in short who we are and what we strive for. At least according to our most recent knowledge. We have given a lot of thought to our being and the meaning of our life and can now easily embrace a few excerpts of our new acquired knowledge.

I am assuming that each of you who have worked conscientiously through this book until now has done so willingly and on your own incentive. It doesn't matter in what phase of life you find yourself, the catalyst was either pure curiosity, interest in assessing your own situation, or most likely because you are willing to change. The reasons for this are, of course, diverse but often have more or less to do with a conscious feeling of dissatisfaction, at least in one part of your life.

Luckily this book doesn't make you succumb to the obligation of choosing a concrete job, a field of occupation or force you to apply for some job, someplace (the lesser of the evils?). Instead, we have formulated our own concrete wishes that will give our life meaning and substance to altogether experience balanced contentment. These are exactly the wishes you will outline in your new calling card. Of course, you don't want to boast and say "Look here, this is me with my wishes and ideas, am I not great?" Instead, simply view it as an indication and challenge for yourself. Use it as a note on your refrigerator, bathroom mirror or as a bookmark in whatever book you're reading at the time. Look at it as our grocery list for what we need the next time we go shopping!

It's best if you start off by copying and enlarging the next page to full size or by typing it up new in your computer. Then take a picture of yourself with the best smiling face you can conjure up. Take it and paste it in the spot marked "Picture of myself". Next, spontaneously circle those three life sectors from the self-fulfillment chart at the end of this book where you believe you are achieving the most fulfillment at the moment (or what you are best at). Work the chart carefully but "from the guts", as usual.

Take your time but don't let your "analyzer" destroy your intuitive choice. Be spontaneous! Write the three sectors down in the spaces allotted for this. For example: How do I feel about my "willingness to accept" (my acceptance capacity) right now? This means: how satisfied am I about my willingness to accept my current situation (how well can I generally accept circumstances?) and so forth. Please pay careful attention to the meaning of the following terms (as given in the chart): Willingness to Accept; Honesty; Relaxation; Finances; Flexibility; Freedom; Leisure time; Health; Hope; Inner peace; Integrity/ Inviolability; Intelligence; intimacy; Career satisfaction: Career status; ability to communicate; Body weight; Creativity; Zest for Life; Life plan; Goal in life; Relationship (partnership); Physical activity; Physical appearance: Self respect; Self-confidence; self confidence; Quality of sex; Quantity of sex; Spirituality (beliefs); Spontaneity; Responsibility; Relationship with your parents; Relationship with your friends; Relationship with your siblings; Relationship with your children; Relationship with yourself; Habitation; Other.

Now take the remaining four areas and in conclusion write down the first step you must take to really experience fulfillment. Actually, you have already answered all these questions. This is just another form of monitoring what you have learned through your notes and exercises to reinforce consciousness!

PICTURE OF MYSELF

MY NAME IS ................................................................ MY AGE ...........................

At the moment I am experiencing THE MOST FULFILLMENT in these three sectors of my life

.................................................................................................................

.................................................................................................................

.................................................................................................................

MY PREFERRED FIELD OF WORK
(I describe here the field of work I will now be active in)

.................................................................................................................

MY POSITION TO STRIVE FOR
(I describe here the position I will now strive to reach)

.................................................................................................................

MY PREFERRED TARGET GROUP
(I describe here the target group I will now approach)

.................................................................................................................

MY DREAM GOAL
(I describe here the goal I want to reach in general)

.................................................................................................................

MY FIRST STEP TOWARDS FULFILLMENT
(I specify here the first step I therefore will – must – now take)

.................................................................................................................

LOCATION AND TODAY'S DATE ...............................................................

Perhaps you remember that you already created a similar "Testimonial" calling card on page 27 of this book. Now you may simply compare that with what you have just written down! There will be some content-related changes and in many cases significantly more clarity and identification.

Naturally, this new calling card can be used later as an excellent tool for self-review. "What did I actually set out to do then and what have I achieved?" It's like a snapshot at this point in time of the knowledge we have learned about ourselves. After your chosen time frame you will be able to measure the effectiveness of your concept. Your results will show just how realistically you have calculated and with how much self-discipline you have been following your life plan to finally reach your life goal.

With these results we will also indirectly find reasons why we were successful (or not) in what we did, how closely we are following our plan, and why or when we deserted this plan (compare with your "Inventory" on page 104). In any case, we will discover that the most predominant reason for this was dependent on our activities and attitude.

In the following chapter I will once again go through all the possible perspectives and aspects to watch for in detail on your path to the meaning of "following your calling". I will show you how to create this path and explain what you need to observe to really find and live out the strived-for position in life, your "purpose in life"!

# 17 | REWARD OF THE JOURNEY: FROM OCCUPATION TO CALLING

This book doesn't want to be the typical advice giver on how to apply for jobs, tailored to giving frustrated job seekers glorified tips how they can best adjust themselves to reach a position that doesn't suit them to later throw in the towel or distance themselves even further from their true being. I want to comment on various situations that we will be confronted with on our way to our personal calling; ones that we don't give much thought to because we are often simply not aware of their consequences. For most people, the path to their own personal calling is found sooner or later through job applications and/or diverse jobs with different companies.

Actually the chain of events always follows the same pattern: We apply for a job, we lead a profession and with luck, we land someplace, sometime in an occupation and position that we can "occupy" capably and with even more luck, come close to our calling. Certainly the majority of people that have not actively taken part in their destiny "only" work at a job and experience their "calling" at best, outside of their jobs. For instance, through a hobby or some other activity outside of work, one that is often only truly discovered after they have retired, unfortunately when their energy is depleted. This doesn't have to be the case and that's why we must be aware of such mundane situations and take precautions accordingly to suit ourselves!

In principle, with our newly found knowledge, we always have a definite advantage over the masses of conventional "job seekers".

We know exactly where we want to go; so on one hand the field we are looking at could have possibly become more extensive since each consciously chosen job is a valuable part of our personal path that better enables us to "endure" a job less than perfect for us. On the other hand we are now looking more specifically because we ourselves become "buyers" in the market, consciously seeking the partner that will support us on our path to finding our "calling".

At the same time we have to realize that there is no patented recipe for these activities. Applying for jobs is always a matter of luck, too! If we are invited for an interview, it is often decided – mutually – if we are suited for each other or not, even if we do not notice it immediately or want to accept it. Naturally, we can always "talk ourselves into" all type of situations, make compromises, lower our standards, make the situation "work", find emergency solutions or choose the lesser of the evils. This applies to employers as well as employees, but we can hardly force luck! The motives of "Pro" and "Con" are as diverse as the human race itself. Just think back on your private experience with people you get to know or want to spend time with.

If we are conscious of this fact we can easily dive into each job interview adventure regardless of how desperately we are in need of a job to finance our perhaps "existential" way of life. We can, of course, always research the company or person, make notes, and maybe use our complete NLP (Neuro-Linguistic-Programming) knowledge to eventually yield to our business partner, however a guarantee for success or favorability is never given. Using precisely this type of otherwise unofficial or confidential researched information can backfire and have exactly the opposite effect of what you were aiming for.

The best recipe for a job interview is authenticity. Be as open and honest as you truly are (with a possible slight "touch" of make-up in the framework of our individual interest in the situation, of course) and enter the conversation by simply listening to what the interviewer wants from you. "Listening" is our device, much like a psychologist listens to his patients. Disclose information on yourself in doses when needed and when specifically asked by your interviewer.

JOB APPLICATIONS ARE ABOUT ADVERTISING YOURSELF ...

... and our job applications and attached documents are for others the first impression of our work, therefore it is advisable to design them clearly, i.e. easy to read in the sense of a "consumer". A trait of good print advertising is simple legibility. Correct grammar and spelling is, in many cases, a must! Depending on the branch and business, you can compose your application with individual features that corres-pond to that field. Basically, the more creative a branch is the more creative your application can be. Of course you will need a good printer if you do not apply by email.

What's important in this respect is also: who is the decision maker? That will be the person we want to send our application to! We can find out who that person is or which department is responsible for ma-king the decision, by simply calling the company and asking them. This question will be of importance when the company declares that they would like to hire you. Here, at the latest, you will finally find out who is in charge. Don't jump to conclusions from the comments of unqualified or uninvolved individuals until you have an official answer, if possible, in writing!

## LESS IS MORE ...

... that's why one page can suffice as an application, unless a major position for a certain subject is requested in the job offer. We respond briefly to the job position and portray our respective qualities in a positive manner (I am qualified because I can...). With a so-called "Unsolicited" application, we concurrently explain what position we are looking for. We explain what type of skills we can offer, regardless if there is an opening available or not. The picture of an "entrepreneur in the enterprise of life" becomes crystal clear here. Actually, this goes without saying for anyone self-employed who wants to submit a good proposal. Many employees simply do not recognize this situation even when they write offers for their employers every day. Short explanations and clear guidelines make it easier for the reader to understand your job application. We must clearly articulate our wish for a job interview, i.e. the chance to introduce our ideas and what we have to offer.

## RÉSUMÉS ...

... are not, in this context, novels but rather information flyers. Ultimately it is about how quickly the deciding party can obtain an overall picture of you. Similar to buying a car; it's like finding out which "features" and what type of extras the "object" exhibits. Does this résumé essentially fit the individual needs or concept of a company? Does it offer a well-rounded picture of the individual, i.e. is it comprehensible? These are the prerequisites before the deciding party goes to the trouble of reading through all the job references. That's why it is best to make your résumé maximum two pages long. The information to disclose in a tabular, chronological order includes: personal information on you and your family, school education and professional background, apprenticeships, jobs, any special knowledge (such as languages), hobbies and so forth. It will suffice to give the month and year you worked for earlier employers (for example: from January 1995 to December 1997, I worked as X ... in the Y ... department of company Z ..., who manufactured W ...).

Specific knowledge is also, for instance, abilities that have obviously had nothing to do with our occupational life till now. As I have said before, they are sometimes, in fact, our only "real" qualities. So include them in the résumé, if they are worth mentioning. Also describe positions positively even when they have not been completed successfully. For example, don't write: left graduate school... Instead write: graduate studies from ... to ...! They should never be placed in a negative light. In the advertising business no product or service is ever presented negatively, either! But remember, you can shed a positive light on everything, but do not lie! They would simply catch up to us at one point, often when we've already forgotten them. Similarly, we have to be honest about the fear concerning our application photo. Now, I know, besides from Germany there aren't many countries that still expect applications with photos. However, if you want to use one, it is worth having quality photos, but most important is the expression of your character. "Natural" make-up can be helpful, as well as good lighting and appropriate clothes. But all these attributes are as subjective as the person who is judging them! We won't be able to appeal to everyone but we will always find someone who finds us appealing. The only advice I can give you is, if you use a photo: "Smile...and the world smiles with you!" Otherwise leave the photo away and let people be positively surprised when they meet you first.

REFERENCES ...

... are well meaning comments about a past relationship. My re-commendation: depending on how often you have changed jobs, it's best only to present the last three (or best three) references in chronological order in accordance with your résumé. If we are especially interested in a position we can present the whole package – as long as it fits your folder – to make an impression. Naturally copies of important certificates (cultural, sports, seminars, workshops) should be included. Otherwise leave these out when sending out your unsolicited application. At first we don't have to prove anything to anyone. If someone wants to see references we'll know soon enough.

In the beginning our reputable name will be enough proof of its accuracy. We only have to prove this when it is implicitly requested and later naturally when we do the job. That's why there can be no lies, only positive depiction. And remember: applying for a job is like the wheel of fortune!

JOB INTERVIEWS ...

... are also there for us to determine if the company suits us. Sure, we've come a long way when we've been invited to an interview after answering a newspaper ad. In the case of an unsolicited application, the job interview will take on more the character of a normal sales conversation. Actually almost every conversation between newly introduced people, who give an account of themselves and their actions, is like an interview. Everyone wants the other person to like them but they also have to reckon with the fact that not everyone is going to like them. We can only know that, at best, afterwards. Go into the interview with self-confidence, but without being pompous and listen carefully  What does the interviewer want from me? Can I "deliver" what they want? Of course we don't have to sell ourselves at any price because if life has a better plan in store for us, we'll know it soon enough. We are entrepreneurs who are discussing the chances for a business relationship with this company.

CLOTHING ...

... is an expression of our personality and how we feel about life. If you stay true to yourself you'll be happy in the long run. In principle what counts is that the clothing fits the occasion! Don't appear as the bird of paradise if you are actually more the dowdy wallflower and only have neutral clothing in your wardrobe and wear these preferably. Although it would be a good idea to evaluate, what your clothing actually says about your attitude towards life.

Sleek clothing and an overall groomed impression belong to a cultivated lifestyle with regard to self-respect and health. This doesn't necessarily mean "expensive" or "new" but comfortable for you and others and appropriate for the specific job or activity. Along with the well-groomed "outfit" goes a positive, open attitude, a peaceful, relaxed mind and body, amongst good manners in the form of respect and politeness, like we would expect from others. If you don't like ties or boring grey flannel suits with pleats, then why wear them? If your contact person is on the same level as you, he will respect the style of others. If not, why would you want to work for them? Stress would only be pre-programmed.

OCCUPATIONAL TRAINING (ATTENTION YOUNGSTERS!) ...

... is basically a manual for industries, trade or other services. There are good and bad trainings and instructors. Despite this, it is also up to the trainee to make the most of it. This wisdom will apply to us for the rest of our lives and will, at one time, catch up with us in some further educational courses. It is our right and actually our obligation, to question any process and – possibly – to improve them. But if we want to change something, we first have to know how it really functions. We should therefore observe our training as a type of basic schooling for a certain economic system and first complain loudly when we know exactly what we are talking about! Then of course become active in the interest of our goals and convictions but skillfully do so with diplomacy and respect. That will get us further. Conviction is the motto, not letting off steam!

Structurally, training programs are basically the same regardless if in the industrial, sales or technical branch but they differ in their details. So if a training program is generally okay, then don't give up on it because of some small symptoms, but be ready to see it through. Whoever wants to get to the top will have to start at the bottom. Be strong with good ideas and if they can't be realized immediately, then write them down and take them with you! You can fall back on them later in connection with a different situation.

OCCUPATIONAL MOTIVATION …

… is becoming more difficult because often there is no identification with the work done. Many are also misled by an unrealistic media-stimulated dream world and we often only work on a tiny part of a complex process without always being able to witness the big picture or the final product. In addition to that it is difficult to motivate someone who is unwilling but we can at least create a motivating atmosphere. This task can only be solved together by employees and employer, even if their goals – superficially regarded – are totally different. When they delve deeper they pretty soon end up at the pursuit of happiness, fulfillment, self-esteem and they discover many things in common.

If we are "employed" by someone we have to basically accept that we are primarily working to fulfill our employer's goals and are being paid for this. There are, though, outstanding business personalities that push others forward and it can be quite satisfying and motivating to work for a good cause – without being the boss – as long as you respect each other and are allowed some freedom. Both sides just have to basically see their common cause.

Of course, good superiors are necessary to communicate (their) great ideas down the line. Unfortunately, they are more likely a rare breed! This is also a wonderful, very individual theme to consider for good management consultancy, which brings me to the next subject:

EMPLOYEES WHO THINK "OUTSIDE OF THE BOX" IN A COMPANY ("MAVERICKS") …
… are valuable staff members who are often the source behind a long term successful company! Constructive criticism is always worth listening to and if businessmen are smart, they will listen closely to what their employees are gossiping about. If criticism is in line or we have suggestions for improvements, simply take note of them even it they cannot be applied immediately. This can also be helpful in officially securing the idea you just disclosed in confidence to your supervisor and to avoid having your idea presented later to the boss as "his" or "her" idea.

Good employers will always honor good suggestions and smart businessmen welcome lateral thinkers gladly – as long as they are loyal – because they most always bring in money. You can compare this in earlier times to the court jester who often gave his ruler important stimulus because they were the only ones allowed to think out loud freely. I like to call myself the court jester for companies I advise, and then I act like one! Especially when someone is new in an institution, the ideas are bubbling over into our consciousness: "new brooms sweep well!" As long as something is new and unusual, we pay attention. But if it gets to be repetitive, we eventually develop "tunnel vision". That's why it is always a good idea to take notes immediately when we notice points of friction. Either we will use them in this company or we'll take our ideas with us to our next employer who is more open-minded. Or perhaps use them in our own company ...!!

EFFICIENCY IN A PROFESSION ...

... is a requirement for peace of mind and satisfaction of the soul. If we have decided to make our manpower available to a firm that doesn't belong to us, but reliably pays us for our work, then we should put forth our best effort as long as we work there and are treated fairly.

Every company could theoretically belong to us at one point and we are part of the business as long as we work there. We carry our mental attitude around with us and if we have "inwardly quit", which means for whatever individual reasons we have inwardly finished with this company though we still continue working there, it is best to leave as soon as possible. Anything less will just feed our frustration and will – worst case – manifest itself in a case of serious illness in our bodies or our relationships.

Ethics ...

... is the doctrine of a universal moral and the standard by which we must measure our actions if we want to be a good role model, to ourselves and to others. If a special phase of your life has come where you want to take a step towards personal reorientation, do not let the past disturb you, neither in dialogue with yourself or when talking to others. It's not worth it, it's a complete waste of energy!

When you interview with a new company or business partner regardless of whether you will be a steady or freelance employee, don't criticize your current or ex-employers. It's best to explain your interest in a change of occupation by using personal and objective reasons. What else do we want to disclose to our future employer? How we're going to badmouth him at our next job interview because we've become smarter? How stupid the others are, how badly we let ourselves be treated, or even what we have planned for the future (unless it's directly helpful for this job)?

No, for when the time comes we will have found a better way. We'll end our job with accustomed quality and without complaining so we can pursue the new path with friendly expectation and without remorse. What's in the past is history ("it's history, baby!"). We were a part of it and we can't change that, so chalk it up to experience that we can benefit from in the future. It made us smarter and more valuable as a person. We have learned from it and this is a gratifying aspect of our life

(YOUR) CALLING ...
... is what life calls out to us to enable us to do the best for ourselves and the whole universe. Even when it is so evident it can still be so distant for most people. Those who have keen senses learn what their calling is, early in life, others only see the signals later, some having to

learn through traumatic experiences caused by making the wrong choices in lifestyle.

Every person has their own individual life clock and the moment to follow their calling, is always correct. There are those however who never discover what their calling is, i.e. what they should do in life to be happy, because they are not willing to use their inherent knowledge. These people are only of interest to us here because they surround us, we must live with them and because they shape the face of earth. Whoever has studied this theme knows that unfortunate people make unfortunate decisions, for themselves and others. And that's how many fatal situations occur, affected by decision makers that have power but no real competence in dealing with a situation. Only think about politicians, their resumes and life content, shaped by hunger for power and political tunnel vision. Many absurd situations will then become clear!

In general, that's why it's worth trying to understand why people are the way they are and ideally support them in their search for a satisfying purpose in life within the framework of their own personal calling. Or otherwise to better remove them from supervisory positions for which they are not suited and could possibly bring harm to others.

In a workshop that I once took part in, the question came up what the actual difference between intelligence and wisdom is. The answer that the leader of the workshop (an American Indian) gave was one that anyone could have given. It still strikes me today as plausible:

"INTELLIGENT ARE THOSE WHO KNOW HOW THEY MUST LIVE LIFE TO BE HAPPY. WISE ARE THOSE WHO ALREADY LIVE THAT WAY."

Let's take this piece of wisdom further to the moral aspect of the categorical imperative (Kant), which is important to me. Remember: "Act accordingly so that the maxim of your willingness at any time can be regarded at the same time as a principle of universal law, without contradiction."

And then, in addition, I would like to offer a definition of "Calling" in the following sentence:
"WE DISCOVER OUR CALLING WHEN WE USE OUR TALENTS AND ABILITIES TO FIND HAPPINESS THROUGH OUR SPIRITUAL, PHYSICAL AND THEREFORE MATERIAL WELL-BEING, THEREBY SERVING A DIVINE PURPOSE IN THE UNIVERSE."

Yet it's not the form of spirituality or ritual of a "God" that is important, but the spiritual essence of love, the core of which all meaningful religions are based on, no matter how they are individually manifested or celebrated.

In the end it's all about finding these respective spiritual qualities in our selves and acting according to the divine role model. Thus the principles of action should always be based on unconditional love. Love your neighbor as you love yourself and let this way of thinking influence your work. Giving, without wanting to take in return or without expecting a reward for our love. Respect and self-respect – perfectly easy!

I was driving in the car once with my that time 6-year old son and asked him (looking into the rear-view mirror) what connection he made with the word "God" and he answered quite spontaneously: "Love! God loves us all, of course!" Now, we really aren't big Church Goers or only halfway bible experts.

He also wasn't crazy about his bible school studies either or the weekly church service in his, admittedly, church-based kindergarten. Moreover, he had definitely never heard this from me directly. Still, this feeling stuck with him and I believe that children all over the world would have given a similar answer. For a moment I could only see the street through hazy eyes.

# 18 | SUMMARY

We, mankind, have all knowledge at our command and everything imaginable in excess, to achieve anything, to be completely happy.

Not always for everyone and perhaps not always right under our nose, but somewhere there's more than enough of everything or at least the possibility to create it. It doesn't matter if it's just the bare necessities, professional or financial goals, dreams of finding a spouse, our health, or our general happiness in life. Everyone has the basic ability in them to achieve whatever it is we really want to accomplish. It depends on our own personal attitude as to what kind of life quality we fill our lives with and what we want to make out of our lives, from a certain point. If we give in abundance, we will receive in abundance. Not everything at once, but in perspective, over the whole cycle of our life. Great dreams and high objectives encourage us to deeds, which promote our quest for adequate significance and our own individual purpose in life, which will bring us the wanted results. We receive from life what we expect from life. A prerequisite for fulfillment in our occupation and our purpose in life – our type of happiness – is our self-honesty. What is really important?

The medium to insight is meditation; deriving inner peace from an individual combination of relaxation and concentration that leads to clarity and energy. For many this is associated with outer silence but others can meditate better under stress. The effect of sincere meditation is an alternative, largely neutral reflection of our life circumstances viewed from our own inner perspective, which enables us to assess our daily thoughts and actions. If necessary, we then alter these to our advantage.

The first steps to a fulfilling life involve the deep analysis and answers of the following three questions as well as our appropriate action. When we have finally reached the point where we can answer "Why" not superficially with material substance but with spiritual content instead:

1 | WHAT DO I REALLY WANT? (My life goals)

2 | WHY DO I WANT THIS? (My purpose in life)

3 | HOW CAN I ACHIEVE IT? (My goal strategy)

Watch the order of these questions exactly because many people, after naming their life goal, have no effective strategy to achieve this and easily fail when the meaning of the connected individual purpose of life is not really completely clear. So first, "What?" and "Why?" will continuously alternate until we finally reach the essence of our personality. The logic cannot end like this: "I want a fat bank account so that everyone will like me". Instead it ends as "I want to reach a significant stage X, so that I can fulfill my purpose in life and accept myself as a valuable human being that I can love, no matter how rich I am or not. My stage X looks like this: …

If our life goal and purpose of life, our individual position and meaning in the universe are recognized, we logically work on a strategy that will lead us on a direct path to a conforming position. Here, in the final steps of the way, the "how" doesn't really matter because our pursuit of fulfillment is unstoppable and knows no permanent frustration even when the original strategy wasn't successful. Goal and purpose are the motivating forces behind our actions!

Further steps and support on this individual path are consistent manifestations of our dreams, thoughts and visions as well as the repetitive affirmation of our targeted goal and life standards. If I have correctly recognized my life goal in one conscious lucky moment, then I will write it down immediately. Through this manifestation I am making my goals constantly apparent so I can reflect on them in less positive moments and be able to evaluate the progression of my goal at a later time.

My faith in a good cause is contingent upon my action and my action is contingent upon my success. I envision this and how I can reach my goal to experience the fulfillment of my life's purpose. In addition, to support my beliefs and encourage my activities, I constantly assure myself with positive words – either verbally or in writing and always in the present tense. I describe myself in the "now", when I visualize the fulfillment of my life's purpose and my aspired life circumstances.

If I believe consciously, I anchor my beliefs and my visions in my sub-consciousness to overcome my doubts whereby my sub-consciousness supports me automatically with all further activities through stored, retrievable knowledge. Faith strengthens my vision, affirmations fortify my beliefs! By the way, typical conventional forms of affirmation are praying and singing!

It this all seems too constructed to you or too complicated, you can simply follow these rules; the effect is the same:

/ Do not concentrate on the problems, but on the chances of an idea.

/ Envision yourself in a successful situation regarding this idea.

/ If you believe in a cause, there will be others who believe in it.

/ Don't believe in "temporary difficult times". Any time has its chances!

/ Don't just concentrate on your known fields of occupation. Use your imagination and be open.

/ Don't let yourself be influenced by personal weak moments. Think about the good times and your good thoughts you had at that time.

/ DON'T GIVE UP! As long as you are convinced of something, keep plugging away until you are successful.

/ Take your dreams and fantasies seriously, shoot for a higher target than "normal".

/ Do things wholeheartedly. What you embody makes you successful and happy – and draws others to you.

/ First of all earn some money. Save some of it and invest these savings in something profitable so when you are well off, you can effectively support the system that once supported you. This doesn't mean this system may not change!

/ Use your talent productively or find your talent in a satisfying existing profession.

/ Shake off restrictive behavior, rigid ideas and be without prejudice towards the unknown.

/ Grasp the chance to use problems and risks as tools for the development of your personality!

/ Create positive experiences without the consumption of worldly goods. Simply be here and now instead of wanting to have everything at once.

/ Be thankful for the simple things. Think positive: "the best things in life are free!"

/ Broaden your horizons for more richness and comprehension, better health and more abundance at all levels of your life.

/ Wherever you go, don 't expect anything but be ready for everything!

If you call to mind on a regular basis all or part of these short guidelines together with the compiled results from this book, the related suggestions, chances and advantages of your unique personality, you will discover that your life will change accordingly.

In each of my workshops or during training sessions I realize how people just don't want to understand or, in fact, understand but are too comfortable to take action, though they have paid me to have their eyes opened. Whoever doesn't make a move, loses!!

Fortunately though, I also do experience how people recognize the situation and act accordingly, making a move. These people are those who make a difference and bring about changes. These people are also those who experience a positive, often exciting turnaround in their life because they have sculptured their life with more intensity and want to live it to the fullest. Because they love their life, themselves and their environment and want to understand it better. Because they feel responsible – at least for their own life! These are the characters on whom I concentrate my energy because only these people are capable of making a vital difference on our earth. And if it only turns out to be one person in one course, then my mission there has been accomplished.

With this book though I want to motivate even more people to do what many think but too few really do: to improve themselves to make the world a better place!

I keep my fingers crossed for all of you or, as my colleague Wayne Dyer says: "I give you all green lights!" on your very own and individual path and wish you lots of wonderful and exciting moments in life and huge success in a self-experienced "following your calling"!

Whoever likes to share their thoughts with me on the stages of their career, tips for others, documentary information, experiences, or accomplishments can write me gladly at the following address: info@lifeangel.de

I look forward to hearing from you and thank you for your interest. Sincerely,


Alexander Teetz

January 28, 2013, 9:46 p.m.

# 19 | MORE MEANS TO MORE CLARITY

Lastly, here is some final, simple advice for clarifying relationships and a guideline for setting up your own personal financial budget.

a) PERSONAL RELATIONSHIP BALANCE SHEET

If you're not satisfied in a relationship, be it personal or business, you should contemplate if, how and why you want to continue this relationship – or not. For this reason, draw up your own personal balance sheet for this relationship noting its PROS (positive features) and CONS (negative features).

Predominantly PRO? Good! Reduce the negative aspects for an even better relationship.

Predominantly CON? Now honestly, what exactly is the original reason? Why (under what circumstances) did you enter this relationship? Can you transform this relationship into predominantly PROS? Do you need this type of relationship at all? What do you really want?

Before you end a relationship, you should keep in mind all the consequences, possible alternatives and their probable development!

By all means this could also be relating to yourself, for example in terms of health, physical or mental aspect.

The first steps to a fulfilling life involve the deep analysis and answers of the following three questions as well as our appropriate action. When we have finally reached the point where we can answer "Why" not superficially with material substance but with spiritual content instead:

# PERSONAL RELATIONSHIP BALANCE

My relationship with ...

PRO (FOR THE RELATIONSHIP)          CON (AGAINST THE RELATIONSHIP)

..................................................................................................................................

..................................................................................................................................

..................................................................................................................................

..................................................................................................................................

..................................................................................................................................

..................................................................................................................................

..................................................................................................................................

..................................................................................................................................

..................................................................................................................................

..................................................................................................................................

..................................................................................................................................

..................................................................................................................................

..................................................................................................................................

..................................................................................................................................

..................................................................................................................................

..................................................................................................................................

..................................................................................................................................

..................................................................................................................................

..................................................................................................................................

## b) PERSONAL BUDGET (EARNINGS / EXPENSES)

Aiming high and having great dreams is good. To get them in line with reality and thus to become successful, most of us need a clear financial status and a clear budget to know where we stand, so we don't already fail in the initial stages of our plan due to a mismanaged financial plan. Below you find a simple plan that will help you determine your income and expenses, enabling you to have a clear comparison on your finances "as is" and, if needed, to help you become debt-free so that you can concentrate all your energy on bigger schemes.

# PERSONAL BUDGET

Calculation period (same for income and expenses!) ........................................
Calculated Currency ........................................................................................................

| INCOME | CURRENCY NET | VAT (%) | CURRENCY GROSS |
|---|---|---|---|
| Non self-employed | | | |
| Self-employed | | | |
| Paid vacation | | | |
| Bonuses | | | |
| Child Support | | | |
| Government Aid | | | |
| Miscellaneous | | | |
| Rent (w/o utilities) | | | |
| Pension | | | |
| Life Insurance | | | |
| Other 1) | | | |
| Other 2) | | | |
| Other 3) | | | |
| Investments (Stocks/Bonds etc.) | | | |
| INCOME SUB-TOTAL* | | | |
| Minus (-) Total Expenses* | | | |
| DIFFERENCE (+ OR - ?) Watch the signs! | | | |
| TOTAL INCOME | | | |

*if the sum of the expenses is always over the sub-total income, we are making a loss, and the difference will have a minus sign. Our Total Income has to be at least more than the Difference or else we will soon be bankrupt. If necessary, we will have to reduce our expenses to at least the amount of the sub-total. Everything that is not necessary or invested in making money has to be omitted!!

NOTE: "ACCUMULATION OF CAPITAL FOLLOWS CONSUMPTION ABSTINENCE!"
(old capitalists wisdom)

| EXPENSES | CURRENCY NET | VAT (%) | CURRENCY GROSS |
|---|---|---|---|
| Rent/Mortgage | | | |
| Property Taxes | | | |
| Gas | | | |
| Water | | | |
| Electricity | | | |
| Garbage collection | | | |
| Personal Liability | | | |
| Insurance 1) | | | |
| Insurance 2) | | | |
| Insurance 3) | | | |
| Telephone | | | |
| Internet | | | |
| Child Care | | | |
| Cable TV | | | |
| Groceries | | | |
| Clothing | | | |
| Household goods | | | |
| Personal grooming | | | |
| Hobbies/Sport/Clubs | | | |
| Vacation/Travel/Fun | | | |
| Continuing education | | | |
| Mobile Telephone | | | |
| Transportation costs | | | |

EXPENSES
**TOTAL EXPENSES***

*carry over to "total expenses" in the INCOME chart

| EXPENSES | CURRENCY NET | VAT (%) | CURRENCY GROSS |
|---|---|---|---|
| Car taxes | | | |
| Car Insurance | | | |
| Car payment | | | |
| Car repairs | | | |
| maintenance | | | |
| Lotto/Cigarettes/Pets | | | |
| Savings 1) | | | |
| Savings 2) | | | |
| Loan 1) | | | |
| Loan 2) | | | |
| Charities | | | |
| Office materials | | | |
| Postage | | | |
| Office furnishings | | | |
| Office rent/utilities | | | |
| Personnel | | | |
| Other | | | |
| Other | | | |
| Other | | | |
| Other | | | |
| Other | | | |
| Other | | | |
| Other | | | |

EXPENSES
**TOTAL EXPENSES***

*carry over to "total expenses" in the INCOME chart

## c) SELF ANALYSIS: FULFILLMENT – "HOW DO I FEEL RIGHT NOW?"

Currently I subjectively experience in the following areas a certain fulfillment that I mark (X) – true to myself – on the following chart from 0 (none) to 10 (very much).

Do I want to improve the level of my fulfillment/satisfaction in these areas I have to identify the necessary quality I have to bring into my life to harmonize it for more individual fulfillment!

| LEVEL OF FULFILLMENT | ☹ 1 | 2 | 3 | 4 | 5 | 6 | 7 | 8 | 9 | 10 ☺ |
|---|---|---|---|---|---|---|---|---|---|---|
| Willingness to accept … | | | | | | | | | | |
| Honesty | | | | | | | | | | |
| Relaxation | | | | | | | | | | |
| Finances | | | | | | | | | | |
| Flexibility | | | | | | | | | | |
| Freedom | | | | | | | | | | |
| Leisure time | | | | | | | | | | |
| Health | | | | | | | | | | |
| Hope | | | | | | | | | | |
| Inner peace | | | | | | | | | | |
| Integrity/Inviolability | | | | | | | | | | |
| Intelligence | | | | | | | | | | |
| Intimacy | | | | | | | | | | |
| Career-satisfaction | | | | | | | | | | |
| Career-status | | | | | | | | | | |
| Ability to communicate | | | | | | | | | | |
| Body weight | | | | | | | | | | |

| LEVEL OF FULFILLMENT | ☹ 1 | 2 | 3 | 4 | 5 | 6 | 7 | 8 | 9 | 10 ☺ |
|---|---|---|---|---|---|---|---|---|---|---|
| Creativity | | | | | | | | | | |
| Zest for life | | | | | | | | | | |
| Life plan | | | | | | | | | | |
| Goal in life | | | | | | | | | | |
| Relationship (partnership) | | | | | | | | | | |
| Physical activity | | | | | | | | | | |
| Physical appearance | | | | | | | | | | |
| Self respect | | | | | | | | | | |
| Self-confidence | | | | | | | | | | |
| Quality of sex | | | | | | | | | | |
| Quantity of sex | | | | | | | | | | |
| Spirituality (belief) | | | | | | | | | | |
| Spontaneity | | | | | | | | | | |
| Responsibility | | | | | | | | | | |
| Relationship with parents | | | | | | | | | | |
| Relationship with friends | | | | | | | | | | |
| Relationship with siblings | | | | | | | | | | |
| Relationship with children | | | | | | | | | | |
| Relationship | | | | | | | | | | |
| Habitation | | | | | | | | | | |
| Other | | | | | | | | | | |
| Other | | | | | | | | | | |
| Other | | | | | | | | | | |
| Other | | | | | | | | | | |
| Other | | | | | | | | | | |
| Other | | | | | | | | | | |

146  NOTES

www.ingramcontent.com/pod-product-compliance
Lightning Source LLC
LaVergne TN
LVHW021502080426
835509LV00018B/2374